I0539171

Our banner is rooted in the events of 1861,
when a pluralist, multiracial, mass movement
birthed a vision for national reconstruction
around universalist ideals. We're calling that
the birth of American Universalism, and it's
why the popular flag of 1861–63 is our logo.

Out of Many, One
Writings on American Universalism

Edited and with an introduction by
Peter Teague, Ilyse Hogue, and Seth Flaxman

Additional editing by Roseann Foley Henry

Published by Catalyst for American Futures, Washington, DC
Copyright © 2025 by Catalyst for American Futures
Copyright © 2025 for individual essays by author of the essay
ALL RIGHTS RESERVED
Design by Shannon Ryan

ISBN: 9798218693688 (Trade Paperback)
ISBN: 9798218702083 (ebook)

Library of Congress Control Number: 2025911580
Title: Out of Many, One: WRITINGS ON AMERICAN UNIVERSALISM

For inquiries or information, please visit our website: www.AmericanFutures.com

First Edition
Printed in the United States of America

Out of Many, One

WRITINGS ON AMERICAN UNIVERSALISM

★

Edited and with an introduction by
Peter Teague, Ilyse Hogue, and Seth Flaxman

Additional editing by Roseann Foley Henry

Contents

★

1   Introduction

SECTION 1

3   The Promise of American Freedom

American Universalism recognizes the core principle of our democracy: The revolutionary idea that we are all created equal, and that from this equality flows the universal right to be free.

4   **Why Universalism Matters—and How It Can Help Us Save Democracy**   By Sam Gill

13   **Plures et Unum**   By Anne-Marie Slaughter

19   **From Universal Light to Individual Liberty**   By Barry Lynn

24   **The Spirit of St. Louis**   By Seth Flaxman

31   **Universalism, Alaska Style**   By Jonathan Kreiss-Tomkins

35   **The America That Will Someday Be a Reality**
By Theodore R. Johnson

SECTION 2

39 America in 2025: Democracy Under Siege

The threat of authoritarianism did not emerge full-blown in 2025. Rather it evolved over the past few decades, drawing our democracy further and further away from its ideals until we reached a point of rupture.

40 **The Gilded Age** By Peter Teague

51 **Make the Presidency Matter Less** By Scott Warren

57 **The Elephant in the Room: Our Leadership Crisis Is Not What We Think** By Judy Estrin

64 **The Future of an American Education** By Michael Sorrell

76 **Authoritarianism Comes to America, Redux** By Sharon Davies

SECTION 3

83 New Perspectives

Each wave of new Americans presents an opportunity to see why the democratic experiment matters so much. Even when America has failed to live up to its promise, we have remained a beacon of hope to the world.

84 **The Promise of Universal Opportunity** By Mari Manoogian

90 **Democracy Must Be Cultivated Early On** By Luis Lozada

94 **The (New) American Dream** By Philippa Pham Hughes

102 **Between Light and Dark: A Gen Z Case for American Universalism** By Hannah Koizumi and Hugh Jones

SECTION 4

107 Universalism From the Ground Up

True universalism starts at the local level, with stronger communities and families, civic pride, and a new focus on education.

108   **The Future Is Engaged Pluralism**   By Jonathon Kahn

113   **Real Freedom Starts with Community**   By Deepti Doshi

119   **Touching Our Children's Hearts With Fire**   By Jason Mangone

SECTION 5

125 Imagining a New American Future

Yielding to tyranny is not an option. There are paths forward—diverse, uncertain, even messy—but we must find common ground. Universalism can show us the way.

126   **I Brought the Flag Home**   By Eric K. Ward

132   **The Research University as a Bastion of Democracy**
By Nils Gilman

137   **Storytellers on Democracy's Front Lines**   By Steven Olikara

140   **When Monsters Are Rampant, Summon Your Heroes**
By Sally Vance-Trembath

147   **The Mosque**   By Shamila N. Chaudhary

151   **Time for a New Synthesis**   By Micah L. Sifry

157   **Fusion of Horizons: Democracy, Identity, and the Art of Holding Differences**   By Ilyse Hogue

164   **The All-American Movement: Strengthening and Saving Democracy**   By John Avlon

170 Contributors

183 Acknowledgements

Introduction

★

In the Gettysburg Address, Abraham Lincoln defined America as a nation conceived in liberty and dedicated to the proposition that all men are created equal. Honoring the devotion of those who gave their lives in a single battle of the Civil War, he also defined the larger and lasting American project. This is the "great unfinished work" that falls to each generation, to ensure "that government of the people, by the people, for the people, shall not perish from the earth."

This anthology brings together essays by 27 Americans—including campaigners, builders, entrepreneurs, journalists, theologians, and historians—who present personal reflections on the universal and radically democratic values at the heart of the American project. We asked them to consider what they mean to us at this moment when an authoritarian takeover threatens to end American democracy.

Given the urgency of our situation, it may seem counter-intuitive to step back and reflect. But these core values have animated every great movement in our history. They inspired the fights to end slavery, recognize women's right to vote, win workers' rights, confront concentrated wealth and power, and defeat Jim Crow segregation. At this time, when the country needs a new movement strong enough to defeat authoritarianism and write democracy's next chapter, we believe it makes perfect sense to remember what inspired the people who came before us, who managed time and again to defy tyranny and move the project forward.

1

The authoritarian right claims to be leading a revolution. Unlike the American and French Revolutions, which paved the way for unprecedented freedoms, this dangerous movement would do the opposite. The threat is deadly serious, and we can already see how the attempt to overthrow liberal democracy is sparking a major reaction from the American people. Accelerating, shaping, and strengthening that reaction is the most powerful strategic response the nation can have. We must counter efforts to divide us and ensure that the people's reaction sparks a pluralist and inclusive movement—uniting a majority around a vision that inspires and helps us believe that "a new birth of freedom," a new and better America, is possible.

We challenged the authors to consider how a commitment to America's universal values can help catalyze that reaction, inspire a new movement, and inform a winning vision. The result is an expression of the American spirit: cultures, experiences, and perspectives that come together to create something new; agreements and disagreements that inform us with nuance and complexity; stories that move and challenge the reader; and ideas that chart a path forward between the alienating extremes of our polarized politics.

It's our time to take on what Lincoln called "the great task remaining before us." We must apply the nation's core values to new challenges, repair inherited faults, and hand the project to the next generation in better shape than we found it. We present this anthology in the humble hope that it will help us remember the simple, radical American idea that we, the many, can also be a single powerful force for good—a people dedicated to the proposition that we are all created equal and free. ★

★

The Promise of American Freedom

American Universalism recognizes the core principle of our democracy: The revolutionary idea that we are all created equal, and that from this equality flows the universal right to be free.

Why Universalism Matters— and How It Can Help Us Save Democracy

What makes democracy work is a commitment to the idea that the things we have in common are as (or more) important than our differences.

BY SAM GILL

President and CEO of the Doris Duke Foundation

While many of us may value plants, animals, and even inanimate objects for more than their instrumental utility, it's clear we feel that there's something that makes humans different. It seems almost axiomatic to say that, absent qualifying context, no person is less deserving than another of at least the right to pursue—if not realize—"Life, Liberty and the pursuit of Happiness."

This distinction is the essence of what is sometimes called "liberal universalism"—that there's something special about humans that inheres in all of us and that confers upon us equal moral status.

Universalism is essential to making democracy work. As the classicist and political theorist Danielle Allen recently wrote, "Democracy is simply a vehicle that empowers people who disagree with one another to try to solve problems together anyway."[1]

Democracy does this through universalism—the fundamental commitment to the idea that, whatever our identities and affiliations, our ability to have them in the first place is the one thing we have in common and therefore the locus of our equal human dignity.

Today, maximalist interpretations of this concept have fallen into disfavor, especially among progressive political movements. Understanding why and how can help to illuminate some of the challenges those movements now face in attaining their political and social aims. And figuring out how to celebrate and integrate universalism into a progressive vision can help to ensure urgent demands for social justice do not descend into a fractious identity politics.

The ancient antecedents of universalism can be found in religious, social, and political doctrines from disparate threads woven across human history. But its role in governing human political communities is relatively recent, at least in what are commonly known as Western European societies.

For most of European history, the default political arrangements conferred special rights on a few and subjected the masses to a level of immiseration we would find shocking today in all but the worst parts of the globe (or of our own societies).

Then, in the late eighteenth century, history swerved.

An accelerating accumulation of social and economic pressures resulted in a series of novel political experiments that began to not simply propose but actually implement some radical ideas: the legitimacy of popular government; the right to believe, speak, and act according to one's conscience, including against the state; the possibility of greater social and economic equality.

---

1 Allen, D. (2025, April) America and Its Universities Need a New Social Contract. *The Atlantic.* https://www.theatlantic.com/ideas/archive/2025/04/stem-academia-universities-citizenship-civics/682384/

Universalism is the bedrock of these ideas, so it's worth exploring just what the notion entails.

One of the simplest expressions of universalism was proffered by Thomas Jefferson in our Declaration of Independence: "We hold these truths to be self-evident, that all men are created equal, that they are endowed by their Creator with certain unalienable Rights, that among these are Life, Liberty and the pursuit of Happiness."

Let's unpack this dense and historically seismic pronouncement:

- Human beings have a rational capacity to determine and pursue what is good for them. This makes people free *("...Life, Liberty and the pursuit of Happiness")*.
- Human beings have this capacity to the same degree, at least morally speaking. This makes people equal *("...all men are created equal...")*.
- The core attributes of this capacity to set our own ends—universality and equality—are objective facts of nature *("We hold these truths to be self-evident...")*.
- This capacity cannot be relinquished. It inheres within us as a facet of our being human *("...certain unalienable Rights")*.

Why was this bundle of concepts so revolutionary?

First, these ideas were posited in societies that were manifestly and profoundly unequal, societies in which the denigration and dispossession of these natural rights was tragically and predictably routine. So these beliefs represented a sharp repudiation of the normative basis of most political communities in existence—and therefore flew in the face of established power (with the full means of the state at its disposal).

Second, these ideas helped us to reconcile a critical tension: that the principal sources of human conflict stemmed from the very capacities that make us human. Bloodshed on a national scale over religious beliefs had become a fixture of the European societies from which these ideas emerged. Universalism provided a pathway to managing disagreements without divesting essential aspects of people's identities.

If, as a matter of fact, we disagree with each other as a result of our innate ability to formulate different ideas of the good, then political society can only be stable by affording the right of all to hold their own idea of the good, irrespective of whether some—including those in charge—agree or not.

In the centuries since, universalism has come in for trenchant critiques, a few of which are worth reprising here because they explain why this idea has fallen into such disfavor, especially in progressive social movements in the United States.

The first is that universalism is a lie.

The proponents of this line of attack argue that there has never been a meaningful commitment to the idea that all people are, indeed, morally equal. The common version of this argument, particularly in the U.S., has been to point out universalism's evidently inconsistent application. From slavery, to the expulsion and extermination of indigenous peoples, to the subjugation of women, to the rise of the carceral state, the history of liberal universalism has been a history of overt and covert, de jure and de facto exclusion of some identity, class, or caste from its entitlements.

The second critique is that liberal universalism masks an anti-universalist agenda.

One of the most incisive and compelling formulations of this line of analysis was proposed by the late philosopher Charles Mills. In *The Racial Contract*, his seminal work on the subject, Mills explored the idea that, while the seventeenth- and eighteenth-century theories that propelled the growth in democratic government represented themselves as neutral with respect to race, they were really only intended to govern White races.

Further, Mills argued that not only have European democratic movements been historically coextensive with colonial domination over nonwhite races, but more provocatively that this civilizational project required the creation and subjugation of a class not entitled to the fruits of subjectivity. That is, Jefferson's (White) man endowed with certain inalienable rights was brought into being by the presence of his negation, the Black man denied any of these rights—denied even the dignity of the faculties that underwrite them.[2]

The third critique—one that is especially popular in progressive circles today—is that universalism requires a kind of epistemic objectivity that just doesn't exist. This idea suggests that my social identity is prior to any individual conception of what's good for me. This means there can be no divorcing my preferences and desires from the influences of context on my sense of self.

This claim may seem arcane, but it has far-reaching implications. First, it suggests that there is no "view from nowhere"—that it's impossible to say something is good for all people, irrespective of their station or social location. Second, it implies further that only an individual or group can have authoritative knowledge about themselves because even an outsider's *internal interpretation* of that knowledge is invariably distorted by their own socially mediated perspective.

This complex notion is actually quite commonly held. Those working in and around progressive social and political movements know this as the argument from "lived experience."

It's important to note that these critiques of universalism have, perhaps paradoxically, been essential in making the application of universalism "more perfect" over time. These ideas powered the global postwar decolonization movements, the American civil rights movement of the 1960s, the disability rights movement of the 1970s and 1980s, and so on. So the point in raising them here is not to refute them, but to seek to reinforce the idea that their application should commit us to more fully pursue universalism, not to abandon it.

But let's look deeper at the analytical engine driving these critiques. What they all turn on is the extent to which group identity trumps individual identity.

---

2   See: Charles Mills. "The Racial Polity." *Blackness Visible: Essays on Philosophy and Race.* Cornell University Press. 1998. See also: Charles Mills. *The Racial Contract.* Cornell University Press. 1999.

Universalism focuses on the individual. The first 10 amendments to our Constitution (the Bill of Rights) accord rights to individuals vis-à-vis the state. Many of our social and political systems negotiate the entitlements of individuals. When we ask about desert—the question of what people are owed—the implied object is usually an individual person in the place of "people."

But what happens when identity as part of a group matters more than individual identity?

The late scholar and political theorist Iris Marion Young wrestled with this question over the course of her career. Young is credited with helping to sharpen our understanding of what we call structural inequalities, which she defined as the condition that "exists when social processes put large categories of persons under a systematic threat of domination or deprivation of the means to develop and exercise their capacities, at the same time as these processes enable others to dominate or have a wide range of opportunities for developing and exercising their capacities."[3] Many of the words we use to elucidate different kinds of structural inequality—marginalization, exploitation, etc.—actually originated in Young's work.[4]

This is the conundrum facing universalism today, a conundrum that has become the organizing axis of a significant cultural debate in this country.

On one extreme are those who seek supremacy for their identity group and cloak that interest in the bad-faith argument that attending to any social differences is a form of discrimination. Clearly this describes at least one faction of the MAGA movement.

---

3   Young, Iris, Marion (2011). *Responsibility for Justice*. Oxford: Oxford University Press. p. 52. Incidentally, Young was my professor and advisor at the University of Chicago in the years before her death (2006).

4   In her landmark *Justice and the Politics of Difference* (1990), Young coined what she called the "five faces of oppression:" exploitation, marginalization, powerlessness, cultural domination, violence.

But even setting aside this powerful, if minority, reactionary view, there is a wide debate within the broader American public culture as well as within progressive movements about whether we are paying *too much* or *not enough* attention to forms of structural injustice—injustice that favors some groups at the expense of others.

Without rehashing decades of profoundly illuminating and challenging scholarly work on the tensions between justice for individuals and justice for groups, there may be at least a few adjustments in how we think about individuals versus groups that can provide more space for the power of universalism to animate a stronger vision for our democracy.

First, groups matter in part because they matter for individuals. At issue in racially motivated police violence is not just the denigration of a group, it is that individuals suffer grievously. An act of racially motivated police violence may harm a racial group—but it also undoubtedly harms a person.

So even a group-based politics can subscribe to the fundamental premise of universalism: that it's what makes individuals the same that most matters—at least morally—in political society.

Second, universalism not only enables pluralism but can itself be pluralistic. As discussed earlier, part of why universalism is so important in a democratic society is that it helps to set the boundaries that enable our differences to express themselves in ways that do not harm others. These differences do not just exist alongside commonly held ideas. They also interact with those ideas, shaping and influencing their quality and sense.

For example, my organization, the Doris Duke Foundation, has invested in building a more prevention-oriented child protection system. Racial disparities in who is involved in the child protection system are well documented. As part of our OPT-In for Families project, child protection agencies pursuing reforms include those with "lived experience" of the child welfare system in their efforts.[5] Although few child welfare administrators share the group experience of those served by the system,

---

5   DDF-OPT-in.org

OPT-In regards their views as a valid and important kind of insight that all stakeholders can understand and incorporate into the policy, administrative, and service structure of child welfare agencies.

Another area in which we work is by providing support to indigenous and tribally led conservation efforts on tribal lands. An important part of this work is drawing on what's called "tribal ecological knowledge." This knowledge, derived from centuries of practice within indigenous communities, plays an important cultural role in these communities. It also works alongside "Western science" to ensure environmental outcomes that can benefit all.

Third, *history matters*. Individuals come and go, but group identities cross generations. Structural injustices can be historically cumulative—individuals can benefit or suffer at the hands of persistent treatment (or mistreatment) with respect to the social groups in which they are included.

What does this mean for the future of progressive movements?

I'd argue that these ideas suggest universalism is not the enemy of justice in a society in which group identities matter, but rather its fundamental aim. We are all morally the same precisely because we share equally in a common capacity for liberty.

We should work to undo individual injustice based on membership in a group when we see it. That work should be a collective endeavor, done by both those who share the group identity and those who do not. And an understanding of those suffering injustice is not a trump card or a quantum of information fundamentally unknowable to those who do not share the group identity. Instead, it represents a special expertise in the nature of the injustice being inflicted.

The way to address group-based injustice is not to ignore differences between groups but to confront them. At the same time, we should acknowledge the common political community in which we are all equal members.

Drawing a line around a human being and abstracting a set of shared, basic capacities—in other words, a common human dignity—changed history. It ended whole classes of oppression and birthed the basic ideas to which we resort today when we fight oppression wherever and whenever it occurs.

In some ways, this is the highest feat of human imagination: our ability to invent an idea that applies to all people who have ever lived and will ever live and that declares immoral even stubbornly quotidian conduct. It's an idea that challenges us to seek a world that has never actually existed as our paramount collective endeavor.

Universalism is not a comprehensive account of our moral status or of the concept and content of justice. But it is a fundamental foundation of just societies that can help us to address persistent social inequality while restoring a sense of shared community and purpose.

More than an affirmative doctrine, ideological movements like MAGA represent a nihilistic cynicism about the kind of diversity our society can tolerate. A renewed universalism can help to turn that cynicism back and restore our faith in the idea that our diversity need not come at the cost of unity, reciprocity, and common purpose. ★

Plures et Unum

Our founders envisioned one nation emerging from many states, but 250 years later we should embrace a new American idea: how to be one and many at the same time.

BY ANNE-MARIE SLAUGHTER

CEO of the think and action tank New America
and global leader, scholar, and prolific author

I am a patriot. When I first described myself on Twitter in 2011, *patriot* was the first word that came to mind, along with *leader, author, mother, mentor,* and various professional qualifications. I borrow my definition of patriotism from Carl Schurz, a Union Army general in the Civil War and later a senator from Missouri, who said: "My country right or wrong; if right, to be kept right; and if wrong, to be set right."

Still, invoking patriotism makes most of my colleagues on the left uncomfortable. I'm not sure why. Perhaps it's the colors. Patriotism is red, white, and blue; my tribe favors black. Not for mourning, but as a badge of sophistication and a staple of urban living.

That's a clue. My friends and peers are well educated and tend to live in cities or university towns, as I do. These are the places where the swirl of nationalities, foods, cultures, and sports allegiances that is such a big part of America is most evident. Blurring all that into a celebration of just one identity seems to erase so much of what makes American life worth living.

So too with flags. My family flies the Stars and Stripes on the Fourth of July, but we also regularly fly the flag of whatever state, country, or even city we are traveling to. (Berlin has a wonderful flag with a bear, as does California.) Flying or wearing American flags has become a marker of conservative or right-wing politics, but it is not clear why. Indeed, when I see an American flag flying today, I hope that it is intended as an emblem of faith in the Republic "for which it stands." I remember reciting the Pledge of Allegiance in grade school and reflect on the rest of that sentence: "one nation, indivisible, with liberty and justice for all." I imagine a future in which symbols of patriotism are markers of unity rather than partisanship.

At the same time, why shouldn't Americans fly our national flag alongside local or state flags, or flags declaring various additional allegiances, such as a pride flag or a flag denoting a specific faith? Most town halls and statehouses signal overlapping geographic identities and loyalties by flying the U.S. flag, the state flag, and a city or town flag. We could go further and fly a world flag, identifying ourselves with all humans on the planet. No one of these identities need deny or subordinate the others.

In my 2007 book *The Idea That Is America,* I recounted a story told by journalist and broadcaster William Harlan Hale about the liberation of Dachau in 1945. He describes the skeletal prisoners, in their rags, looking for any bits of cloth they could find to make crude national flags for a liberation ceremony with the troops of various nations.

The Americans came last; Hale describes the commanding officer as a "tall, gray-haired colonel" who climbed the platform "and spoke a few words of greeting and fraternity." Three American soldiers then marched in, a color guard, carrying the American flag. They moved toward the platform, and Hale thought they would climb up and mount the flag above all the others. "But at the last moment," he writes, "they wheeled toward the assembled thousands, carried our flag into their midst, and placed it there with the banners borne by men in convict stripes from a dozen victim peoples."

The moment defined America for Hale. As he came away, he thought: "This is what we mean, this is what we are." For me, imagining this moment decades later, it is a vivid demonstration of American universalism. We are not above other nations, but with them.

★

American Universalism is embedded in the self-evident truths set forth in the Declaration of Independence: all men (not just American men) are created equal, and endowed with unalienable rights. Of course, Jefferson actually meant only White men, and he was not using "men" as an umbrella term for "human"—women were excluded as well as men of color.

Still, the creed of equal creation and equal rights for all men of any category, across social and geographic lines, was revolutionary for the eighteenth century. It was self-evident in most societies that men were born *un*equal, into castes or classes that determined the arc of their lives and circumscribed the narrow ambit of any rights they might possess.

I draw a line—albeit a crooked, wavering one—from our Declaration of Independence to the Universal Declaration of Human Rights, adopted overwhelmingly by the United Nations General Assembly in 1948. Eleanor Roosevelt chaired the drafting committee, which was composed of eight additional members from France, China, Lebanon, Chile, the Soviet Union, the United Kingdom, Canada, and Australia. Many of the world's great civilizations and religions were absent, or more accurately, represented only by their imperial governors. Even so, the United Nations could now credibly declare that the eighteenth-century rights of man now belonged to all the peoples of the globe, by virtue of their humanity alone.

My patriotism is grounded in American Universalism, but I recognize and embrace the paradox at its heart. It is American universalism, but it is also French universalism; French revolutionaries issued the Declaration of the Rights of Man and the Citizen in 1789. It is the universalism of all the nations who signed the Universal

Declaration and later signed the two great implementing treaties on civil and political rights and economic, social, and cultural rights. By definition, universalism cannot belong to one nation alone.

Even within one nation, universalism must coexist with pluralism. It is about one and many at the same time. *One*: Our common humanity transcends our differences. All humans are created equal and have equal rights. *Many*: humans come in many shapes, skin colors, cultures, clothes, and faiths. Those differences give rise to associations of like with like. Accepting and embracing that diversity is the heart of pluralism.

More profoundly, pluralism recognizes our groupness in the same way that universalism recognizes our separateness as individual human beings. The eighteenth-century Enlightenment philosophers who informed the thinking of our Founding Fathers were all men. They lived in a world in which care and the nurturing of deep connection was women's work. That division of labor limited their understanding of human nature in a way that contemporary neuroscience, biology, anthropology, sociology, psychology, and natural history all challenge.

If we define human beings consistently with our actual physical and psychological needs, we see that belonging is as important as self-actualization. Our relational identity, as a member of a family, tribe, community, or chosen group, is as important as our individual identity. Isolation literally kills us; connection enables us to thrive.[1]

That is the foundation on which we can and must rebuild our commitment to universalism. While we affirm that all human beings are created equal and enjoy equal rights, we must also establish the responsibilities that come with those rights, the duties that attend our liberties, and the care and connection that offsets competition. With a deeper understanding of human nature, pluralism and universalism can balance one another.

---

1   See Elizabeth Garlow and Anne-Marie Slaughter, "A Worldview of Care & a New Economics," *Dædalus* 154, no. 1 (Winter 2025): 206–223, https://doi.org/10.1162/daed_a_02133.

★

I travel a lot. When I come home from an overseas trip, generally through Newark Liberty International Airport, I always smile and feel a thrill of pride at the sheer range of faces, races, accents, and personalities waiting in the passport lines with me. These are my fellow Americans, in all their energy and exuberant difference.

When I look up, I see a looping video on a mounted screen that welcomes us home, with pictures of the equally diverse beauty of the American landscape: plains, mountains, bayous, deserts, and forests. And then the people. A farm family from the Midwest, which makes me think of the warmth and generosity of the Iowa family who welcomed my Belgian mother as a high school exchange student in 1953. Big city parades, family reunions, baseball games, monuments, and meals. As many times as I've seen it, I always get a little choked up.

These are clichés, I know. They are belied by the millions of deeply divisive videos that I could spend the rest of my life consuming on the Internet. Any newsfeed I open will quickly remind me of all the forces in contemporary American life that lead us to put politics above people, enmity above unity. But the experience of all that difference, so striking after the relative homogeneity of the countries I have visited, all while standing in the line that designates us as Americans rather than visitors, captures the contradictions that define us.

We need a new American idea. The Continental Congress adopted the Great Seal of the United States in 1782 with the inscription *E Pluribus Unum* (out of many, one). The committee charged with designing the seal included Benjamin Franklin, John Adams, and Thomas Jefferson. They wanted a motto to symbolize the coming together of the 13 colonies into one nation.

Today we should focus less on the states of the United States and more on the people. In 2026, the 250th anniversary of the Declaration of Independence, we should modify the motto to reflect our simultaneous unity and diversity, our universalism and pluralism. Over the course of the twentieth century we moved informally from melting pot to multi-culturalism, but neither fully captures who we are.

Let us embrace the patriotism of *Plures et Unum* (many *and* one). We can be—we are—both at the same time. Let that understanding of universalism, with pluralism at its core, define us for the next 250 years. ★

From Universal Light to Individual Liberty

The struggle for freedom of the soul four centuries
ago holds lessons for today's liberal democrats,
in our own fight against autocracy.

BY BARRY LYNN

Executive director, Open Markets Institute

Like many people, I started my own journey toward a deeper understanding of liberty and democracy by reacting against something. In my
case, this was the concentration of power, control, and capacity in the
United States and around the world that resulted from the dismantling
of antimonopoly law in the 1980s and 1990s under presidents Reagan
and Clinton.

My work as a journalist helped me to see how this radical change in
policy—and ideology—had undermined the stability of our industrial and
financial systems, the distribution of opportunity and responsibility in
our political economy, and true equality in American democracy. I knew
I was *against* all these things. I knew I was *anti*-monopoly, *anti*-oligarchy,
anti-mercantilism. But in the early stages of my fights against monopoly I
didn't spend much time pondering what positive vision inspired me.

Twenty years ago there were still many people—especially economists and the executives at corporations that had captured monopoly power—eager to defend the idea of monopoly. Concentrated control was efficient, they said. It delivered lower prices. In response, I would detail some of the many harms caused by monopoly. I showed how monopoly led to higher prices, lower quality goods, and lower wages. I showed how it made it harder for entrepreneurs and skilled workers to keep their independence, and how it drove concentration over the news media and politics. I even showed how monopolists increased the chance of war, as their new chokepoints created dangerous temptations to coerce or exploit other nations.

Obviously, implicit in each example of what I fought *against* was some idea of what I fought *for*: peace, prosperity, choice, opportunity, democracy, liberty. But these goals in turn raised other questions. Especially the word *liberty*. What do people want liberty to do? Why?

On finishing my first book, *End of the Line*, I knew I'd done something important. I had detailed how concentration of risk had made a complex system—the international production system—subject to catastrophic failure. I'd also shown how to use law to engineer such systems—even when they are composed of thousands of companies and millions of people each making their own decisions—to prevent any such crash.

I also knew that I had begun to crack the code of language and ideology the monopolists had originally used to justify and sell extreme concentration of power and control. And so I consciously set out to recover and refine the language of antimonopoly, or rather, the language of liberal democracy.

By the time I finished my second book, *Cornered*, in 2010, I'd succeeded in moving the discussion beyond how monopoly harms us as consumers to how it threatens our interests as citizens. How, for instance, it limits what sort of human beings we might become, as corporations captured control over entire lines of science, entrepreneurship, craft, and business that had once been open to all. How monopoly undermines our democratic institutions and our voice in politics.

But once again, I knew my journey was incomplete. In *Cornered* I still wrote of liberty largely in the negative, as freedom from certain forms of power and control. I still had not discussed how to make a soul free, or what a free soul might seek?

In this search, I was not personally constrained by any religious structure. My mother's family traces to anarcho-syndicalist Jews from a city now inside the borders of Belarus, and my dad's to the Little Flock Baptist church in Lynntown, Georgia. I grew up in Miami in a room shaded by a mango tree.

In my most recent book, *Liberty from All Masters*, I aimed to finish my journey back to first principles, first thoughts, first dreams. Practically, this meant moving swiftly past all the technical conversations about the purposes of the Sherman Antitrust Act to look instead at what antimonopoly principles and goals Americans had distilled in the Constitution and Declaration of Independence. And to understand the lessons of the English Revolution of the seventeenth century, the great historical event that loomed over America's founding generation.

For most Americans, the word Puritan conjures images of control, coercion, the one right way to worship and live. And if we look at life in the Massachusetts Bay Colony, this is not far from the historical record. But this specific truth about this one community hides a broader truth about Puritanism and Protestantism in Britain and America—that in this rebellion against the established church we find many of the origins of our own society's vision of individual dignity and liberty. We also find here much of the language and rules by which we understand and construct our individual souls and our common democracy.

The idea that Puritan settlers in Boston aimed at theocracy is right. They sailed to America seeking liberty to establish an unfree society, in the form of a "godly utopia."[1] They fled a policy of general toleration of Elizabethan England, where to keep the peace among the many sects of

---

1 William Haller, *The Rise of Puritanism*, New York, Columbia University Press, 1938, page 189

believers the Queen had established a broad right to preach as one wished, but not to impose.

Most everywhere outside of Boston, however, we see something radically different, as Puritan debate helped to foster not theocracy but revolution. During exactly the years covered by Hawthorne in *The Scarlet Letter*—1642 to 1649—in the camps of the New Model Army and in formal debates in St. Mary's Church in Putney, soldiers and other plain folk proposed a new popular constitutional system of government, centered on near universal male suffrage, freedom of conscience, self-ownership, full equality before the law, and democratic representative government.

It was a revolution driven largely by a new belief in the spiritual equality of all people, which came straight from the mouths of the preachers. As the historian William Haller put it, in preaching that "none were righteous," the Puritans had led "ordinary" people to conclude that "one man is as good as another."[2] It was a revolution driven also by the practical education offered by the preachers, as common people "learned to read, to use a book, to exchange ideas and experiences, to confer intellectually after their own fashion upon common problems, to partake of the exhilaration of discussion and self expression."[3]

It was a revolution that also swiftly reached across the ocean, with the revolutionary government in London granting a charter for a colony in Providence, Rhode Island, that guaranteed both democracy and absolute separation of church and state. This broke the monopoly of the Massachusetts Bay Colony and ended the experiment of American theocracy.

During these years, there were many great preachers of liberty, both men and women. Few were as sophisticated as the poet and pamphleteer John Milton. In 1644, Milton published *Areopagitica*, a polemic against censorship of the press and of speech. The essay is of value as a description of the effects of such control on both the individual and society, as

---

2   Ibid., page 89

3   Ibid., page 63

Milton warns of how control over the press shall "bring a famin upon our minds again, when we shall know nothing but what is measur'd to us by their bushel." The essay is also of value in answering the question of what liberty makes possible, which is, well, everything. Or in Milton's words, a great cacophonous community of thought, as individuals engage in "disputing, reasoning, reading, inventing, discoursing, ev'n to a rarity, and admiration, things not before discourst or writt'n of."

In 1667, long after the restoration of monarchy and of top-down rule, hence after the collapse of the republic Milton had fought to create and protect, he published *Paradise Lost*, an epic poem in which he replayed the intellectual and political battles of the English Revolution, through characters lifted from the Bible, in verse. Feeling much the same despair we do as we behold the attempts by President Trump and his oligarchs to impose autocracy upon us, Milton distilled all the spiritual and political lessons of decades of struggle into an observation by Adam, one that would ring through the decades to 1776: "Man over man' God made not lord; such title to himself/Reserving, human left from human free."[4]

Many Americans today recoil from essays that tread near questions of religion and spirituality. So I'll end with words from Christopher Hill, the great Marxist—and atheist—biographer of Milton. We should never let our modern "skepticism," Hill wrote, "reflect back upon the fantastic daring of the seventeenth-century thinkers who expressed their hard-won belief in the importance of human beings through the medium of theology."[5]

Thus perhaps we can relearn a core lesson of almost every religion, which is the true spiritual equality of all humans. And thus, perhaps, also relearn one of the ultimate ends of spiritual liberty, which is to turn back to the political world fully armed to protect the laws and systems of liberal democracy for all peoples in the world today, and the worlds to come. And this means, practically, breaking every effort to impose monopoly control over our pocketbooks, jobs, political beliefs, imaginations, and souls. ★

---

4   Christopher Hill, *Milton and the English Revolution,* New York, Viking, 1978, page 382
5   Ibid., page 305

The Spirit of St. Louis

At the darkest moment in American history,
a coalition with deep divisions united to defeat
tyranny and change the course of history.

BY SETH FLAXMAN

Social entrepreneur, democracy activist, writer,
and co-founder of Catalyst for American Futures

★

Like a lot of American Jews I was raised on the warning: It can happen here. After the attempted coup on January 6, 2021, I recognized that it was happening but felt lost about what to do. So I did what often brings me inspiration: I looked to history to understand what we've done in other times of darkness.

I had a particular moment in mind. In his 1860 campaign, Lincoln introduced the language of "universal freedom" into our political discourse. To many, the language must have seemed naive and hypocritical. Far from naturally dying out, as many in the founders' generation had imagined 70 years earlier, the "slave power" was ascendant and expanding. I imagined the Americans committed to universal freedom at that moment, Black and White, living in an anti-slavery city as secession-mania took over their slave state. Where were they and what did they do?

They lived in St. Louis, and what they did was wilder than I could have imagined. It is the true story of a coalition that came together in 1861 to defy tyranny and—against all odds—to win.

Here's the scene: St. Louis was three times the size of Chicago at the time, and mostly populated by Germans and Austrians—who despised each other. Anglos called them all "the Dutch." The first immigration wave of the so-called Dutch was conservative and religious (Catholic, Lutheran, and Jewish). They hated the second wave, known as the 48ers, who had led a failed revolution in 1848 to overthrow the German princes and install a constitutional republic. They were a bunch of condescending, over-educated liberals and leftists, and of course this second wave also all hated each other. The leftists blamed the liberals for their failed revolution, the liberals blamed the leftists, who were literal compatriots of Marx and Engels. They both blamed and despised the Catholic Church, so you can probably guess why they alienated the city's Irish. And the Irish weren't the only Catholics in town either.

The self-declared "Colored Aristocracy" of St. Louis was almost entirely Catholic, with French-colonial roots that predated the Louisiana Purchase. Cyprian Clamorgan, a member of this aristocracy, wrote a book profiling its members two years before the Civil War. At the center of the community was likely the richest Black woman in America, Madame Pelagie Rutgers. An entrepreneur and widow, she had purchased her freedom before marrying one of the largest landowners in the city, a free Black man who had inherited massive tracts of St. Louis from his father, a Dutch enslaver. The Colored Aristocracy owned property and businesses, and Cyprian writes about how this wealth empowered them to build the Republican Party in St. Louis. They had no voting rights, but as major landlords and purchasers they controlled a decisive share of votes.

The nation was paying attention. St. Louis was nationally proclaimed the "fortress of freedom" by the Black press, the radical German press, and Anglo Republican papers. The city was in constant battle with a state government ruled by what these papers called "the slavocracy."

Our story begins with the start of campaign season in May 1860, when the Republican Party in St. Louis launched its first statewide campaign ever in a slave state. They would run a candidate for every statewide office, with Lincoln at the top of the ticket, despite everyone's ambivalence. None of the St. Louis factions had supported Lincoln, and the Republican National Convention had pulled the factions farther apart. German Marxists were even removed for disrupting the convention with their demands for a more forceful anti-slavery position.

Yet before Lincoln and the Republican statewide candidates could legally be printed on ballots, they had to check a procedural box: They had to hold a public meeting in St. Louis to nominate and ratify their slate of Republican candidates. The public meeting was met with textbook political violence, with a pro-slavery mob attempting to stop the ballot ratification.

The attack not only failed, it backfired. The thousands of Republicans attending the rally held off the mob until the ratification process concluded, and the next day, leftists and liberals put aside their grievances and decided to bring back a political club the Germans had founded more than a decade earlier. It had also been born from political violence, organized to defend polling places after a nativist Know Nothing mob had burned one down in the early 1850s. The club had only lasted a few years, as political infighting tore it apart. They relaunched now with a new American brand: They would be called the Wide Awakes. It was mostly, but not exclusively, German.

One of the men who joined the Wide Awakes was Antoine Griveaud, a 20-year-old French-Catholic. He was the adopted White son of Madame Pelagie Rutgers. Alongside his adopted German-Catholic sister and their Black sister (Madame Rutgers' biological daughter, Antoinette), they formed the multi-racial Rutgers family. You can read more of the family's hard-to-believe history in an autobiography by Antoinette's husband, *From Tennessee Slave to St. Louis Entrepreneur: The Autobiography of James Thomas.*

The family had everything at stake. If the slavocracy gained ground in the November state legislative elections, they had promised to confiscate Black wealth and enslave free Black families.

So with Republican candidates successfully ratified, campaign season launched with impossibly high stakes. Antoine was active that summer. He likely wore a Wide Awakes fireproof cloak and cap and carried a six-foot oil lantern as he joined his compatriots in forming protective rings of light around Republican rallies. The Wide Awakes marched to these rallies in silent columns, receiving drill instruction from volunteer Army vets, including a washed-up Ulysses S. Grant selling firewood from a cart.

That campaign season would see more political violence. To illustrate how the city had become a den of sin under Republican control, the same men who had attacked the ratification meeting in May razed 20 dancehalls, taverns, brothels, and boardinghouses in the harbor district around Almond Street, killing two police officers who resisted. Almond Street sounded like their version of the Castro District in San Francisco. I imagined myself living there, wearing the silk hats and patent leather boots that James Thomas writes about being trendy at the time, albeit "only suited to dandies." (Spoiler alert: This neighborhood is also where my novel takes place.)

Again the violence backfired. That November, Republicans lost statewide but swept everything in St. Louis: every state legislative seat, sheriff, and schools chancellor. In the most competitive congressional district in the country, they elected the only Republican Congressman in a slave state: Frank Blair (who had previously served in Congress as a Democrat, before the Party kicked him out for not being pro-slavery enough).

Yet Republican high spirits quickly collapsed after the newly elected Governor let his mask drop in his inauguration speech. Despite having won as a moderate pro-Union Democrat, the governor was now committed to secession.

The next day the governor's allies in the state legislature introduced bills that seized control of the St. Louis police, confiscated Black property to fund the Missouri state militia, and made criticism of the governor punishable by death. As these bills were introduced, a militia arm of the slavocracy revealed itself in St. Louis: They called themselves the Minutemen.

Then Congressman Blair received a tip: The head of the Missouri State Guard had circulated a secret order among the Minutemen to seize the federal arsenal of weapons in St. Louis when all the Catholic church bells rang. St. Louis had the largest arsenal outside Washington, and whoever controlled it controlled the city, the state, the Mississippi, and the West. Congressman Blair wired the Buchanan administration for support, but Buchanan didn't believe him, and some cabinet members were complicit. The city would be on its own for two months until Lincoln was inaugurated on March 4.

Congressman Blair called on the Wide Awakes; left, liberal, and conservative Germans; Yankee business leaders; and the Colored Aristocracy to fight together against impossible odds. As Cyprian Clamorgan had foreshadowed in his book just two years before the crisis, Frank Blair was one of the White men who "can always depend upon" the free Black community "in any emergency." And when the emergency did come, James Thomas wrote that of the "old colored Catholics," notably "the women were if anything busier than the men."

Their coalition faced down this and four more plots to take the arsenal. Each plot was discovered and defeated, but just barely. And as the city lay under siege, refugees poured into St. Louis from across Missouri, targeted by roving militias for flying the American flag. Many likely brought their flags with them—often bearing the popular design of the time: 34 stars arranged in a circular shield.

The leaders in this coalition hated each other personally and were ideological opponents with racial and religious prejudices. Yet they worked together because of the common threat of tyranny. How did they win? They moved fast, they innovated, and they stuck together by focusing more on what united them than on their many stark divisions.

They wielded political power, defeating, delaying, and watering down bills in the state legislature through parliamentary maneuvers and speeches that divided their opponents.

They wielded economic power, as the Colored Aristocracy joined forces with business leaders including the Anheuser-Busch family to put their wealth and reputations on the line.

They wielded people power, shutting down the last attempted trade in human beings in St. Louis by occupying the public square, with the new sheriff's quiet support, making it impossible to continue.

They wielded media power, keeping the city informed in multiple languages. They kept printing when the legislature tried to shut them down, and they kept publishing as the Minutemen tried to burn down both Anglo and German newspaper offices.

They wielded cultural power, organizing in beer halls and defying the state by putting on shows at the German Opera House on Sundays—at least until the state completed its takeover of the St. Louis police board and shut them down by force.

They wielded legal power, buying time in the friendly St. Louis County courts.

They played politics inside the Army chain of command, getting three traitorous senior officers removed from the arsenal's defense.

When the coalition discovered itself under surveillance, they hired every private investigator in the city to keep tabs on the spies outside their homes and ran two separate spy rings, mostly powered by networks of Germans and Black Americans, both free and enslaved.

And of course they continued to vote, mobilizing record turnout for a last-minute February election to determine delegates for a state convention on whether to secede.

The coalition thought the crisis had ended when it split the vote of pro-slavery delegates at the state convention, getting some to vote against secession. Instead, the Governor gave up on electoral legitimacy altogether. He mustered the Minutemen into the State Guard and amassed his army inside a city park, determined to take the arsenal and secede by force.

Five thousand of the city's Home Guards—the Wide Awakes all grown up—mobilized overnight. They had received secret training from another vet, William Tecumseh Sherman, the president of the 5th Street omnibus company. Surrounding the park, they forced the Governor's militia to surrender.

The city's forces, now under federal command, swelled to 14,000; they encircled St. Louis in a protective human wall and stormed the state capital by steamboat, chugging past sabotaged railroad bridges and forcing the Governor into exile. Missouri remained bitterly divided, but the tyranny of slavocracy never recovered.

Now we are in different times, of course. This is not a call to storm state capitals by steamboat! But our forebears have some lessons for us:

Their victory relied on pluralism. Their coalition was cross-ideological. Capital and labor, interfaith, stretching across cultural, racial, class, and educational chasms.

They were resilient, fighting on every front and never giving in to despair. They were pragmatic and strategic, acting in time to matter.

They had less time, fewer resources, fresher divisions, and steeper odds, and as they worked together, they birthed a vision for national reconstruction around universalist ideals that can still serve as our North Star. They did not debate whether to spend time fighting fires or building positive visions of the future—they built the future out of the fires.

Yes, it can happen again, it can happen here, and our history shows the way forward. This is the root of my patriotism and the source of my hope. I see Americans stirring to action. I have faith that American Universalism is our nation's destiny. I believe that freedom will win. ★

Universalism, Alaska Style

There may be no better example of how universal opportunity makes a difference than the annual, equal sharing of the state's oil wealth with every resident.

BY JONATHAN KREISS-TOMKINS

Fellow, Institute for Responsive Government, and
five-term member of Alaska Legislature

I grew up in a small island town in Southeast Alaska called Sitka. Sitka is not some national political hotbed. But thanks to the wonders of the 56-kilobyte dial-up Internet, I became obsessed with electoral politics at an oddly young age.

I dabbled in some political campaigns in high school and got fully hooked. After a few years in college, I was getting antsy to do something in the real world. When an opportunity arose to leave college early and come home to run for the state legislature, I went for it. The district, which included my hometown of Sitka, encompassed an archipelago of remote communities, mostly consisting of Native villages and fishing and logging towns. I ran against the Republican incumbent. I caught him flat-footed and barely won—by 32 votes.

The Alaska Legislature is how I cut my teeth in politics. The subsequent decade-long chapter in the Alaska capitol gave me a healthy appreciation for my state's abundant political idiosyncrasies.

Most states like to think their state's politics are unique. I'd argue that Alaska's really, truly are.

The exemplar of Alaska's unusual politics is the Permanent Fund Dividend, affectionately known as the PFD. There's nothing like it in the country. In fact, there are few if any peer programs to the PFD anywhere in the world.

You may not have heard of the PFD because, outside Alaska, it is probably best known in wonky left-of-center and/or libertarian circles. The PFD is a kind of accidental, miniature version of universal basic income (UBI) in which every Alaskan gets a check every year as their share of the state's oil revenue. Most Alaskans have never heard of UBI. They just know the PFD as the annual cash transfer that pluses up their bank account and triggers a slew of annual "PFD sales" at eager businesses across the state.

Alaska made a ton of money after the discovery of oil and the completion of the Trans-Alaska Pipeline in the late 1970s. Governor Jay Hammond, a Republican in the Teddy Roosevelt mold, believed everyday Alaskans should share in the state's newfound oil wealth—a belief rooted in Alaska's constitution.

Thanks to a governor and legislative leadership who took the long view, 25 percent of oil royalties were socked away in a sovereign wealth fund called the Permanent Fund. Money makes money. As of today, 45 years later, the Permanent Fund is worth $80 billion.

It took a few legislative false starts and a high-profile U.S. Supreme Court case, but the PFD ultimately became law, and the first checks were distributed to Alaskans in 1982. Every eligible man, woman, child, grandmother, and newborn received a $1,000 PFD check that year ($3,391 in inflation-adjusted 2025 dollars). The program has continued ever since.

Today the PFD is getting the squeeze, as Alaska's elected leaders struggle to resolve the relationship between the Permanent Fund, an adequate level of public services, and broad-based taxes (more accurately, the lack thereof). Put mildly, the politics of the PFD are complicated. But at least for now the PFD exists. For as long as the PFD exists, it remains a broadly beloved Alaska institution, especially among working-class and rural Alaskans.

Setting aside the question of American Universalism for a moment, there may not be a better example of *Alaskan* universalism than the PFD. It is as universalist as it gets: Every Alaskan, regardless of race, class, or creed, receives the check. Getting a PFD means you're Alaskan. There is no means testing, no restrictions on how the money can be spent.

Some Alaskans use it to buy big-screen TVs or other glitzy consumer items. Some capitalize on Alaska Airlines' annual PFD fares to buy plane tickets to Mexico or Hawaii. Many kids' parents sock away the money in a college fund, which turns into a hefty nest egg by the time high school graduation rolls around.

Whatever each Alaskan chooses to do with the money, the PFD is a great, uniting—one could say universal—aspect of being Alaskan. There is a sense of ownership and dignity and togetherness in receiving the check.

My view on American Universalism is informed by the fantastic success of universalism that is the PFD. I love things that unite us as Americans and create shared, foundational experiences. We don't have enough of them. We need more.

The success of the PFD has made me a student of this version of universalism in other countries. Ever heard of Finland's baby boxes? All Finnish parents—poor or rich, Helsinki urbanites or northern Sami reindeer herders—receive a cardboard box from the Finnish government that contains essentials for newborns: clothes (including impossibly cute baby snowsuits), toiletries, and a Finnish picture book titled *Lystileikit vauvan kanssa* ("Happy games with a baby"), among other items.

National service (cf. Israel or Singapore) is another example of universalism that fascinates me. I've long hoped that our country would take strides in this direction. I am closely following and rooting for Gov. Wes Moore's service-year program for Maryland high school graduates and hope it inspires similar programs at a greater scale.

I wonder how the broadly shared (though not quite universal) experience of the draft and World War II shaped the Greatest Generation.

Sacrifice became a common, shared experience. (Far too many made the ultimate sacrifice.) How did service and sacrifice shape this generation's views towards their country, neighbors, and fellow citizens in the decades that followed?

It may be too easy for me, a Millennial, to interpret their sacrifice through a halcyon lens of history and Hollywood, but I think it nets out as positive in some powerfully foundational way. The attitudes and norms that were forged by my grandparents' generation seem ever more distant and faded. All that seems to have taken its place is influencer culture and TikTok algorithms.

How can we rekindle the shared sense of "us" that we've lost over the past century—to find new cornerstones of universalism? We are in desperate need of a movement (not a world war) that will pull us together more powerfully than algorithms and demagogues push us apart.

To me, universalism means something literally universal. It may not ultimately be a yearly check (though I would be excited if that were to come to pass), but we must find ways to tangibly reforge a common American identity and recreate a shared American experience. ★

The America That Will Someday Be a Reality

Patriotism does not mean excusing the country's errors—it means having the will and determination to correct them.

BY THEODORE R. JOHNSON

Contributing columnist for *The Washington Post* and senior advisor, New America

More than two centuries ago, the newly founded United States faced the first test of its values and resolve in the waters just beyond the New World. Pirates on North Africa's Barbary Coast had been demanding money from American merchant ships, raiding the ones that refused to pay and selling their crews into slavery. In response, the young nation quickly raised a Navy, decisively won the Barbary Wars, and found one of its earliest heroes in the daring commodore Stephen Decatur. At a victory banquet held in his honor, Decatur delivered an iconic toast: "Our country! In her intercourse with foreign nations, may she always be in the right—and always successful, right or wrong."

James Thompson, a cafeteria worker at a military aircraft factory in Kansas, held a different idea of patriotism. Writing to the *Pittsburgh Courier* after the United States' entrance into World War II, he criticized the country's hypocrisy in fighting tyranny abroad while subjecting Black Americans to it at home: "I suggest that while we keep defense and victory in the forefront, that we don't lose sight of our fight for democracy at home." For Thompson, honoring the country meant calling it out when it errs, not being proud when it does wrong things well. He championed the creation of a Double V campaign: "The first V for victory over our enemies from without, the second V for victory over our enemies from within." Anything less than equal access to democracy and opportunity invites the question Thompson famously poses in his letter, "Should I sacrifice my life to live half American?"

I learned Decatur's quote while in training at the Navy's officer candidate school. Its patriotic sentiment and example of heroism at sea held just the sort of spirit the drill instructors sought to cultivate in us aspiring sailors. I'd joined while in college after the service had implemented new recruitment programs to diversify its nearly all-White officer corps, offering stipends and job security after graduation to Black college kids like me. The love of country in the quote felt familiar, but the finishing flourish—*always successful, right or wrong*—was something I could never drink to. In the same decade Decatur gave his toast, an African man named Kincey was sold into slavery in the United States. He was the great-grandfather of my grandmother, a Georgia woman born in 1915, in the same year and county where seven Black men were lynched without trial or due process, treated half-American.

I understand what it's like to feel both proud of, and disappointed in, the United States. Our country—when right, and when wrong.

That is not a declaration of nationalism, which can excuse intolerance, injustice, and inequality. Nor is it uncritical patriotism, believing that there is only room for celebration and loyalty and none for critique and accountability. Rather, it is a proclamation of belonging and agency. It means we each have ownership and a duty. True patriotism, like democracy, requires enough of Decatur's pride to fiercely champion America's place in the world and enough of Thompson's capacity to acknowledge the shame in the nation's longstanding shortcomings. The measure of America is not whether it is successful no matter its endeavors, but whether its endeavors, successful or not, are in the right. And whether we correct them when they are not.

It is a project that requires all of us, from every rank and station of American life—something made clear during my military service. I worked and deployed and hung out with men and women hailing from every corner of the country. It was an education in just how much Americans have in common, despite our differences, and in the distinctions that make us a nation distinct from all others. But I was also a Black man in an American outfit, part of the same institution that refused Harlem-based regiments in World War I from fighting under the American flag and made them into French forces instead. I took an oath indicating my willingness to die for a country that has permitted all manners of injustices against people because of their race or immigration status or gender for longer than it has not. Here, there are always things to be proud of and ashamed about. Pluralistic societies embrace both pride and critique; unjust and anti-democratic ones force a choice between them.

For the American experiment to succeed, it requires a people who can hold pride and shame together. The country is a far better version of itself today than at its founding—we should be proud of that. Many worked tirelessly, some giving their lives, for that progress to be possible. The country has harmed many people, too, forsaking its values for its interests and political expediency—we should be ashamed of those choices. Pride reassures us that our work to improve the country is a worthy and achievable cause; the shame grounds us to our values and principles, serving as a check on our actions and intentions.

But whatever the country does, it is ours. We, not fate or destiny or providence, own its actions. Patriotism means undertaking those responsibilities seriously. Pluralism means doing it with compassion for others. A more perfect union requires our active participation and not shrinking from either duty, especially when the country is in the wrong.

It is said that the United States is the first nation founded on an idea—one encapsulated in our establishing document: that we are all created equal; that we have inherent rights to life, liberty, and the pursuit of happiness; and that government derives its power from the people. In this light, the finishing flourish of Thompson's letter could also be a national toast and a call to heroism. *I love America—and am willing to die for the America I know will someday become a reality.* Whether a young officer candidate or an aspiring pluralistic patriot in an imperfect nation, I'd drink to that. ★

★

Democracy Under Siege

The threat of authoritarianism did not emerge full-blown in 2025. Rather it evolved over the past few decades, drawing our democracy further and further away from its ideals until we reached a point of rupture.

The Gilded Age

Over the past century we have seen how democratic government can lift families up and provide opportunities for success. We've also seen what happens when government tilts the scales in favor of the powerful.

BY PETER TEAGUE

Co-founder and senior advisor, Catalyst for American Futures

★

This year marks the one-hundredth anniversary of the fire that took the lives of my grandmother Della and her eldest child, the 16-year-old boy who would have been my Uncle Alden.

I want to tell a little of Della's story and a little of mine, then offer some thoughts on what connects our stories with America's story, and finish by suggesting a possible way out of the crisis we're now in.

Della Estelle Griffin Teague was born in 1890 in America's Gilded Age. She married at age 15 and by the time of her death at age 35 had nine kids: eight boys, including my dad, and one girl, my Aunt Neva. Della never heard a radio. She never owned anything more than what could be carried in a mule-drawn wagon. None of the rented houses she lived in had electricity, plumbing, or paint. Like most country women she only ever saw a doctor when she was ready to deliver.

Many decades after Della's death, Neva wrote down her memories of her mother from the time of the fire. Neva would have been ten at that time, and my dad eight.

Neva writes:

She had a beautiful singing voice. She was one of the soloists when the older boys and their friends would gather at our house to play various string instruments, sing, and "buck dance." I don't know how much education she had—maybe 6th or 7th grade. She loved to read. I don't know where she got books and reading material. Many times when Cecil would get his nap, she would prop up in bed and read.

It was one of those nights when the neighbor boys were there, when our house burned—August 26, 1925.

The boys were in the front bedroom with their friends. Papa, Mama, and the little kids were playing in the other room where Baby Cecil was asleep in the bed. Alden was trying to repair the gasoline lamp that lit the room. The lamp exploded.

Alden ran through the joining bedroom where the other boys were playing music. The boys said he was a ball of fire. He was running as fast as he could out the door and down the hill. Ralph caught him, and the skin was already blistered and slipped in his grip. One of them grabbed a quilt, ran him down, and rolled him in the quilt to put out the fire. I heard later that he swallowed the blaze.

Mama came back through the fire to rescue Cecil. Her clothes and hair caught fire. The room was big and we four kids were standing watching the fire on the other side of the room. She rescued Cecil from the bed and told us to follow her.

Hoyt Hamilton was outside and when we emerged he put the fire out on Mama and I remember his patting the fire out on the top of her head. We went around the house to the front yard, and Alden came up to us. He was naked and asked Mama where he could get clothes. She asked someone to find a bedsheet and then draped it around him. That is the last time I saw him alive.

Papa took Mama and Alden to Birmingham on a freight train that came through town about 10:00 p.m.

Mama came home in about a month. She stayed in a room at the old Odenville hotel. I'm not sure if it was free or if Papa rented it. She had a special nurse but developed bedsores.

The nurse applied iodine, and she died from iodine poisoning.

Neva's account makes me feel as if I'm looking into a different universe. Though I grew up with these stories, it's hard to believe that was life in America in my parents' generation: no electric lights, running water, fire extinguishers, phones, 911, fire department, or EMTs—just a late-night freight train to the nearest doctor.

★

DEVELOPMENT, DEMOCRACY, AND FREEDOM

In a book called *Development as Freedom*, Indian economist and Nobel laureate Amartya Sen articulated the profound connections between democracy and human development; both are concerned with increasing freedom by expanding people's choices and capabilities. Sen argues that democracy is not just a political system but a crucial tool for fostering human development and well-being. He writes that the two are inseparable and are, in turn, inseparable from political, economic, and social freedoms, which are universal, interconnected, and mutually reinforcing.[1] Sen's conception of democracy wraps political theory around what some of America's greatest leaders have seen: for people who have no property, money, or education, political freedom alone is an empty concept.

---

1   Sen, AK. (July 1999) "Democracy as a Universal Value." *Journal of Democracy.* https://www.journalofdemocracy.org/articles/democracy-as-a-universal-value/

Sen's concept of development is the story of my family and my country. Della's America was a developing nation. Whatever freedom she had to make choices about her own life was, to say the least, limited. She was pregnant and nursing almost continuously from age 15 to her death 20 years later. While my grandfather did whatever he could to earn an income—he was at different times a coal miner, peddler, and sharecropper—Della raised the kids who were needed to farm the land and, ultimately, support elderly parents. She grew and cooked the food; washed the pots, pans, and dishes; bathed the babies; and laundered the clothes (which she had also made). To do all of that, she had to carry water in gallon lard buckets up the long hill from the well.

My America has made available to me choices that would have boggled my grandmother's mind. I was free to choose the education I would get, the careers I would have, the person I would marry (regardless of gender), where I would live, how many kids I would have, the spiritual path I would take, and the places I would travel. As I sit here writing on my laptop, glancing out the window at San Francisco Bay, with my Brazilian husband downstairs on a Zoom call talking to art students from around the world, I can see the path of human development that connects my life to Della's.

Eight years after my grandmother's death, FDR inaugurated the New Deal, and for the first time the South's poor had a government that worked for them. The Tennessee Valley Authority brought electricity, industry, and jobs. The government aimed numerous programs at revitalizing the depressed economy, providing relief for the poor and protections for workers and farmers, preserving the environment and folk culture, and advancing the diversification of state economies.[2]

Those New Deal programs demonstrate the validity of Sen's point. They didn't end the Great Depression, and too many of them adhered to morally bankrupt Jim Crow racial policies. Still, for my family and millions of others, it was the government that accelerated the process of

---

2 "New Deal in Alabama." *Encyclopedia of Alabama.* https://encyclopediaofalabama.org/article/new-deal-in-alabama/

human development. By expanding the choices we could make and the capabilities we could develop, those programs made the nation's core values—equality, freedom, and opportunity—a lived reality for the first time. Except for Alden, Della's boys all served in (and survived) WWII. My dad became a naval officer and commanded ships in the Mediterranean and then, in a later war, Korea. When they returned home, the brothers took advantage of more government programs, including the GI Bill and federal home loan guarantees, to build middle-class lives.

My parents raised me in California when the state was investing in the foundational infrastructure—schools, universities, parks, transportation, water, and road systems—of what is today the world's fourth-largest economy. I grew up with good public schools and great public universities. The modest amount of in-state tuition my parents paid, and the money I earned from part-time jobs, was enough for me to earn two degrees without going into debt. I served my country as my dad and uncles had, but in my own way, with two years in the Peace Corps and five on Capitol Hill.

★

POLITICAL RIGHTS ARE NOT ENOUGH

The government-powered escalator my family rode from rural poverty to middle-class comfort demonstrates the idea that American democracy works when it is a thick package of political, economic, and social freedoms. Political rights alone are not enough. My grandmother may have had the right to vote in the last four years of her life (the Nineteenth Amendment was ratified in 1920), but whatever political freedom she had was undermined by the vastly unequal world she lived in.

Things were worse for Della's Black neighbors. Henry and Mary Gross and their several kids, and Martha Washington and her son, Luther, would have risked being lynched for attempting to register, let alone vote. And while New Deal projects expanded the meaning of democracy to include economic and social freedoms, most were compromised by forms of structural racism that operated to exclude Black people.

For centuries, some of our greatest leaders have argued that the nation's democratic promise could only be achieved by extending the whole package of political, social, and economic freedoms to Americans regardless of race and gender. In the 1850s, Frederick Douglass wrote about the relationship between economic inequality and political democracy, insisting that true political freedom is only possible under conditions of material equality.[3]

In the 1960s, civil rights leaders demanded a "New Deal for Black America,"[4] arguing that the social and economic policies that had lifted my family were as vital to the health of democracy as formal political rights. Once those were secured with passage of the Civil Rights Act of 1964 and the Voting Rights Act of 1965, Bayard Rustin and A. Philip Randolph (the key organizers of the 1963 March on Washington for Jobs and Freedom) refocused their pursuit of racial justice with a universalist strategy of broad-based economic reforms. They sought to build an expansive coalition with labor unions and other White-led groups based not on shared identity or oppression but on common economic and political goals.[5]

MOVING IN THE WRONG DIRECTION

This universalist strategy has been called the "unfinished march" because its key demands—full employment, affordable housing and health care, and high-quality public education for everyone—have not been fulfilled.[6] In fact, the unfinished march—what Sen would identify as the change needed to catalyze and expand the process of human development—has been edging backward and is now in danger of going into full retreat.

3   Karp, M. (Feb. 2020) "Frederick Douglass Railed Against Economic Inequality." *Jacobin.* https://jacobin.com/2020/02/frederick-douglass-railed-against-economic-inequality

4   Fong, B. (Summer 2023) "The Jobs and Freedom Strategy." *Catalyst.* https://catalyst-journal.com/2023/08/the-jobs-and-freedom-strategy

5   Ibid

6   "The Unfinished March." Economic Policy Institute. https://www.epi.org/unfinished-march/

For decades, politicians from both parties have been dismantling democracy by dismantling Americans' economic and social freedoms. Their political and economic project has siphoned wealth, opportunity, and liberty from the many to the few and replaced America's flawed commitment to freedom with an ideology that valorizes wealth and power. They have opposed efforts to expand the programs that lifted White families like mine to include nonwhite families, arguing that government itself is now the problem. Demonstrating what Yale historian Timothy Snyder calls the politics of inevitability,[7] they insist that markets and technology—godlike, not to be interfered with—are the solution.

These powerful ideologues have encouraged disinvestment in public goods and government capacity, unprecedented concentrations of power, and the rise of private government. They pushed trade deals that closed factories, sent jobs overseas, and destroyed communities. They attacked union organizing and public education. They fought for financial deregulation and met the resulting financial collapse with bailouts for bankers. They waged wars they had no strategy for winning and looked the other way while powerful corporations pushed drug and social media addictions.

Unfortunately, people's rage and frustration with these moves have been better understood by American authoritarians than by supporters of democracy. These authoritarians pose as populists, champions of the working class, claiming as their goal the overthrow of a corrupt "deep state" to deliver a new golden age for "real Americans."

What they actually intend is revealed when Donald Trump explains what he means by "make America great again." He says that he's thinking of the Gilded Age. That's when Trump believes the U.S. was at its peak. "We were at our richest from 1870 to 1913. That's when we were a tariff country."[8]

---

7   Berkowitz, R. (March 2022) "The Politics of Inevitability." *Amor Mundi.* https://hac.bard.edu/amor-mundi/the-politics-of-inevitability-2022-03-20

8   "President Trump Remarks at Republican Governors Association." C-Span.org, February 20, 2025. https://www.c-span.org/program/white-house-event/president-trump-remarks-at-republican-governors-association/656015

Three decades ago, my dad wrote his account of that time, the Gilded Age of his youth:

"The Civil War had wrecked the South, and the federal government had done absolutely nothing to help beleaguered families. Heavy tariff was imposed on all products going north or south. Young families without farms became sharecroppers to the large landowners. As far as my family was concerned, along with most other young families, we could eat dirt, and that is about what we did."

The Gilded Age that Trump admires was an era of vast concentrations of wealth and power in the hands of a few wealthy businessmen. Industrial tycoons such as Carnegie and Rockefeller had enormous control over political institutions. Meanwhile, most Americans lived in my family's world of grinding poverty, rampant disease, and an almost complete lack of freedom. Tariffs could fund the federal government because the federal government did almost nothing for its citizens. "The most astonishing thing for historians is that nobody in the Gilded Age economy—except for the very rich—wanted to live in the Gilded Age economy," says Stanford University historian Richard White.[9]

The sad irony is that people, and young people in particular, report higher levels of confidence that the right wing's phony populists will protect democracy than centrist liberals.[10] The right has delivered a convincing narrative that speaks directly to the experience of a broad swathe of Americans across racial, ethnic, gender, and generational lines. The story acknowledges regular people's frustrations with the consequences of policies that self-styled centrists in both parties have advanced—offshored

---

9 Zeitz, J. (March 2025) "The Gilded Age Is Back—and That Should Worry Conservatives." Politico.com https://www.politico.com/news/magazine/2025/03/02/trump-musk-bezos-gilded-age-corporations-economy-00205454

10 Lewsey, F. "Faith in Democracy." University of Cambridge. https://www.cam.ac.uk/stories/youthanddemocracy

jobs, hollowed-out communities, forever wars, economic collapse, bank bailouts, Covid-19 lockdowns, opioid addiction. It offers villains, victims, and a hero. It is spoken in plain, fuck-you English. And Trump, the guy who tells the story best, proved he was serious about it by destroying the more centrist GOP establishment. That's how he delivered a clean break from all the bad stuff and earned voters' trust.

Trump's opponents, on the other hand, have lost that trust as they have lost the plot of the American story. From the beginning, the American project has been about opposing tyranny in the form of concentrated wealth and power and building, as a countervailing force, a liberal democracy that serves the interests of the many. President Franklin Roosevelt argued that it was a constitutional necessity to overthrow the "economic royalists" and build a "democracy of opportunity" for all Americans in the economic and the political spheres.[11] According to scholars Joseph Fishkin and William Forbath:

> Arguments in this tradition hold, broadly, that we cannot keep our constitutional democracy—our "republican form of government"—without (1) restraints against oligarchy and (2) a political economy that sustains a robust middle-class, open, and broad enough to accommodate everyone. The most important and compelling arguments in this tradition hold that (3) a constitutional principle of inclusion—across lines such as race and sex—is inseparable from the first two requirements, and equally necessary for sustaining the political economy that republican government demands.[12]

---

11 Acceptance Speech for the Renomination for the Presidency. The American Presidency Project, UC Santa Barbara. https://www.presidency.ucsb.edu/documents/acceptance-speech-for-the-renomination-for-the-presidency-philadelphia-pa

12 Fishkin, Joseph, and Forbath, William E. *The Anti-Oligarchy Constitution: Reconstructing the Economic Foundations of American Democracy* (p. 3).

This broad vision, anchored in the universalist values expressed in the founding and every great social movement in American history, can draw the support of majorities and even supermajorities. How do we know? Because Trump and his vicious party ran on it and won. They increased their margins with virtually every group of voters from 2020 to 2024. The lies they tell now about their intentions—that they support Social Security and Medicare; that they won't touch Medicaid; that they are taking on the elite enemies of regular Americans by rooting out waste, fraud, and abuse, and making America more free and more prosperous— tell us how powerful the universalist vision is.

This shamelessly dishonest project should have been easy to beat (in fact, the authoritarian victory should never have been possible in the first place). But when his opponents talked about "democracy," voters didn't believe them. They had helped drain the word of its full and proper meaning, defending the procedures, norms, and institutions of a system that no longer works for people. Instead of staying focused on completing Randolph and Rustin's unfinished march and updating the vision for today's realities, elements on the left became the right's accomplices: the center by going along with (or leading the way on) policies that have wreaked havoc on regular people; the progressive left by wrapping even their best policy proposals in the language of a divisive ideology that has alienated voters across every demographic.

Our job now is to pick up the story where patriots like Douglass, Tubman, Lincoln, Anthony, Roosevelt, Brandeis, Randolph, Rustin, and King left off. We have to commit ourselves to a fully inclusive version of the "thick" democracy that lifted my family out of Gilded Age poverty and gave me the freedom to choose my own life. That's it. That's the project. We can argue about trans athletes, assault weapons, climate change, and Gaza once we've figured out how to win by remembering who we are and what our story's about.

MAGA will fail to solve the problems it promised to solve. It already has, and its failures will accelerate and multiply. In the chaos and violence that are likely coming, we need to build the capacity to gain the initiative, wedge their coalition, unify ours, and turn MAGA's strengths into weaknesses and our vulnerabilities into strengths. We must create a home for the growing number of Americans who are disillusioned and discouraged and want to act, but who don't see a banner they want to identify with or rally around.

Together, we need to define in broad terms what the universalist project means for us now and then build a convincing case that we can make it real. This is not the moment to develop a fully fleshed-out vision for government or a preferred set of policies. That is the work of a pluralist process of debate, negotiation, and compromise among Americans who come together to defeat authoritarian rule. The work of this moment is to build a majoritarian movement that can provide Americans with a clear choice of visions: MAGA's twenty-first-century version of Gilded Age oppression and misery, or its opposite, a new vision of freedom grounded in America's universalist values.

I like the idea of Della being free to make her own choice. ★

Della Estelle Griffin Teague, c. 1915, likely pregnant with my dad, John Wesley Teague (one of two photos that survived the fire)

Make the Presidency Matter Less

The path toward recovery requires a rebalancing of government into equal branches and redistributing power back to where the founders imagined it.

BY SCOTT WARREN

Fellow at the SNF Agora Institute at Johns Hopkins University

My late grandfather, Sidney Warren, was a presidential historian. I like to think he was a great historian, but you probably haven't heard of him. He was both Jewish and legally blind, which was a somewhat lethal combination for climbing the ranks of academia during his tenure.

Despite those real barriers, he was prolific. Throughout his career he interviewed figures like Harry Truman, Herbert Hoover, Eleanor Roosevelt, and JFK's famed advisor Ted Sorensen. In August 1960, my grandfather wrote a piece in the then-influential *Saturday Review* magazine entitled, "New Dimensions in the Presidency." In it, he argued that the president of the United States was becoming as much the leader of the free world as one focused primarily on domestic issues. He noted that, "the American Presidency is a unique office. It can be compared to an elected kingship, a repository of both pomp and power."

Shortly after publication, he received a copy of the article in the mail from a reader, and my family has kept it ever since.

"This is the greatest article I've read on the greatest office in the world," read a note on the article. The reader scribbled his signature: Harry S. Truman.

My grandpa died months before Barack Obama was elected, although he was following that election with great interest. I often reflect on what he would have thought about the presidencies of Donald Trump. A repository of pomp and power indeed.

With my grandpa in mind, I argue—hopefully with his approval—that for the sake of American democracy, the office of the presidency itself must matter less. The American presidency must matter less to policy. The presidency must matter less to culture. The presidency must matter less to us.

In recent years, the presidency has come to occupy too much of our collective consciousness, but this is not a recent phenomenon. Indeed, in his 1964 book, *The President as World Leader*, my grandfather posited that, "The nation has come to look to the White House for an immediate answer to any and all significant problems." This sentiment has undoubtedly worsened in recent decades.

More than 156 million Americans cast ballots in the 2024 presidential election, but tens of thousands of citizens, from just a few states, effectively selected the winner. President Trump, with little resistance from a completely subservient Congress or an acquiescent Republican party, has claimed a total mandate. He has completely upended the global economy, unilaterally changed our immigration policies, disobeyed court orders, closed executive agencies, bulldozed through the federal bureaucracy, and usurped cultural institutions throughout the country. He has acted, in my grandfather's words, like an elected kingship.

But it would be unfair and unproductive to completely blame the current administration for this new reality. Previous Democratic administrations have engaged in their own version of expanding the role of the executive from a policy and culture perspective. This is not to engage in both sides-ism, but rather, to attempt to provide an accurate overview of the problem.

President Obama began the Deferred Action for Childhood Arrivals (DACA) program in the midst of the 2012 election cycle, allowing undocumented individuals who came to the United States as youngsters to remain in the country. Irrespective of the merits of the policy, the fact that it happened without Congressional authority has led to the policy being in a limbo since its inception. Obama also vastly expanded military action, including the use of drones and an incursion into Libya, without Congressional authorization.

The Biden administration continued this pattern, including its efforts to forgive student loans, which was struck down by the Supreme Court. His excessive pardons of family members at the end of his term also proved an exception to previous presidential norms and laid the groundwork for future abuses of the system.

The inflated role of the presidency is also not just the fault of presidents. Congress essentially does not do its job and has slowed to an essential partisan halt. As an example, the 187th Congress (1961-62) passed 1,095 public laws. The 118th Congress (2023-24) passed only 274. In the 1960s and 1970s, 30 to 40 percent of bills were passed with bipartisan approval, and almost all budget bills were passed on time. The opposite is true now. The current Congress has demonstrated no interest in either legislating or standing up for its role, deferring completely to the president's agenda.

Nor is the elected kingship reality just the fault of institutions. The American people have largely stopped paying attention to local politics and put all their hopes, dreams, and worst nightmares in the office of one person. While many on the political right now see Trump as a political savior, the same could have been said about Obama during his tenure. Media coverage was fawning, and rallies revealed near-religious devotion to a man depicted as more than that in the infamous "hope" drawing.

Additionally, although only a handful of voters in a handful of states decide the presidency, Americans largely eschew local elections, despite the fact that local governments are much more responsive to their everyday lives. Approximately 64 percent of eligible voters participated in the 2024 general election, but only 15 to 25 percent of Americans vote in local elections in off-years.

This obsession with the presidency is not sustainable. If a Democrat wins the White House in 2028, they will spend their first months of 2029 signing executive orders unwinding the efforts of the Trump administration while rebuilding a decimated federal workforce. This action might be necessary to restore order and democratic norms, but the cycle needs to be disrupted at some point.

The presidential obsession is also not healthy: many Americans' mood and behaviors are tied into the actions of one person. Each election we hold is billed as the most important election of our lifetimes.

Such an obsession is dangerous. The more power the presidency has in our collective politics and culture, the more it enables the potential presence of authoritarianism itself.

Decreasing the power of the presidency is complex, and establishing that as the end goal should not diminish the serious harm the Trump administration has already done to our institutions, and may continue to inflict over the next four years. Defense is needed at the moment.

Additionally, the argument about the potency of the presidency should be taken separately than that of the importance of the executive branch of government. The progressive battle of ideas between a more Jeffersonian form of government, in which power is devolved, and a more Hamiltonian form, in which a strong central government makes decisions, should continue to be contested. Exploring whether a less regulated government or a strong federal bureaucracy produces the best results is a debate that should continue.

But that debate is separate from the question of the president's position. We all stand to gain from an approach in which the president matters less. There is an opportunity for a political movement that appeals to all Americans to focus more on their immediate surroundings, and less on one occupant of the Oval Office.

My own career has included founding and leading a K-12 experiential civics education organization and subsequently convening and organizing conservatives to build trust in elections. These are seemingly disparate efforts, but the throughline is an attempt to focus civic efforts away from the presidency and towards local politics.

In high school classroom discussions, the first impulse of students would often be to attempt to tackle issues like gun violence or climate through writing letters to the president. Through our curriculum, we encouraged students to focus on local action, even picking up the phone to call their local council members, who would take their concerns seriously. Students felt more empowered and less cynical about politics when they realized their local elected officials were real people.

Similarly, when we gathered groups of election administrators and legislators in states across the country in 2024 to focus on a conservative pro-democracy agenda, participants were almost desperate to focus on local politics, away from the presidential campaign. As Wyoming participants told me, "Undocumented immigrants voting in Wyoming elections is not a thing, but it's all anyone is talking about because of Trump."

So what do we actually do? An agenda to de-emphasize the presidency would be far-reaching, and could be completely universal in nature. From an institutional perspective, it would involve focusing on ensuring that Congress was more effective, which may necessitate changing the body's incentive structure and how members are elected (and potentially even growing its size). It would also necessitate a bipartisan effort to curb executive power. It could be useful to have the next president come into office with an explicit desire to make their position matter less. While it may seem counterintuitive for a future office holder to want their office to matter less, state governors might have a useful perspective to bring to the table both because of their experience leading locally and holding front-row seats to local issues becoming disruptively nationalized. In 2029, it will have been 20 years since a governor was in the White House. (In our nation's history, there has been only one longer period in which a governor was not in charge: between FDR's presidency's end in 1945 and Carter becoming president in 1977.)

Another important step could entail actions citizens could take to de-emphasize the power of the presidency. Increased civics education could encourage a renewed push to participate in local elections. We could ensure that we are subscribing to local news outlets and paying attention to local issues.

And perhaps most importantly, we can get involved. There's been a renaissance of thinking on the importance of place-based work. Historically, this has involved joining local clubs and organizations, like church groups, or local branches of Rotary or NAACP. We can reimagine what this looks like in creating new forms of local bonds and institutions. Civic culture could flow upwards, rather than defaulting to the national.

It may seem counterintuitive at a moment in which an authoritarian leader is seemingly intent on destroying democratic institutions to focus *less* on the presidency. But in the long term, it may be exactly what our democracy needs. It's a perfect time for what my grandpa called "new dimensions in the presidency." ★

The Elephant in the Room: Our Leadership Crisis Is Not What We Think

Silicon Valley leadership styles have
infiltrated politics, culture, and business.
Naming the problem is the first step to reversing
the shift to authoritarian and chaotic leadership.

BY JUDY ESTRIN

Networking technology pioneer, Silicon Valley leader,
and author of *Closing the Innovation Gap*

★

In November 2008, a broad range of business, professional, academic, and civil society leaders gathered at the California Academy of Sciences in San Francisco to celebrate the launch of my new book. Even amid the financial crisis, optimism filled the room. The election of President Obama, bringing his leadership capacities, felt like a breath of fresh air: inspiring and deliberative, strong and collaborative, and open-minded, with an appreciation for encouraging critical thinking, the humanities, and scientific discovery.

Today among the crises we face is a crisis of leadership. Understanding the breadth of this problem is key to adequately tackling our other challenges. As with so many other aspects of our digitally infused lives, our concept of leadership has been flattened, focused solely on charismatic personalities. Leading requires the ability to build a following, but in the end, it is about problem solving—removing obstacles that stand in the way of progress toward an open, free, and resilient society.

The shift to the authoritarian and chaotic leadership we are experiencing did not begin with Trump. Silicon Valley did much to set the tone with its "move fast and break things" and "scale fast or fail fast" mantras. Swept away by the benefits of digital services—real and promised—and blinded by worship of innovation, wealth, and scale, we did not pay attention to how much the values of Silicon Valley had shifted away from those we were celebrating that evening in San Francisco. With a frenzy around artificial intelligence[1] and the Trump/Musk strongman effect in full swing, we must develop alternatives to a maximalist leadership culture and the incentives that got us here. To lead the country forward, our response to strongmen must be to leverage a strong core—nuanced, stable, and elastic strength—concomitant with periodic martial arts moves to turn their aggression to defeat them.

The first of historian Melvin Kranzberg's six laws of technology—"Technology is neither good nor bad; nor is it neutral"—is why the values of those developing and wielding tech are so important. As digital platforms proliferated, a winner-takes-all environment in Silicon Valley guided business and product decisions. The tech leaders coalesced around the values of *dominance, disruption through deconstruction,* and *removing all friction[2]*. The early networking industry's open system innovation, which encouraged interdependence, was replaced by vertical integration making it harder to counter Big Tech's rule. I wrote my book, *Closing the*

---

1 Estrin, J. (Aug 2023) "The Case Against AI Everything, Everywhere, All at Once," Time.com https://time.com/6302761/ai-risks-autonomy/

2 Estrin, J. (April 2019) "I Helped Create the Internet, and I'm Worried About What It's Doing to Young People," *Pacific Standard.* https://psmag.com/ideas/i-helped-create-the-internet-and-im-worried-about-what-its-doing-to-young-people/

Innovation Gap, to voice my concerns about a lack of research funding, and that we were not planting the seeds of innovation. A decade later, the growth of the innovation ecosystem metastasized[3] and turned inward as leadership in the Valley drifted toward authoritarianism[4].

While political leaders became more influenced by (the worst of) Silicon Valley, tech leaders borrowed from authoritarian playbooks with promises of utopia and inevitability narratives, at the expense of their constituents (users). Technology *will* march forward toward less friction and more convenience according to their vision of the future. Digital platforms provided the tools to undermine trust, truth, agency, and critical thinking. Our information ecosystem has been hijacked[5]—encouraging absolutism and overriding nuance.

They mirrored authoritarian populism. Promising to democratize and raise up voices, they created a digital state of nature in which the loud minority has the algorithmic edge. Disintermediation, "removing the middleman," was heralded as empowering for the people, when often it actually served to consolidate distributed gatekeeper power to the platform algorithms. The same goes for making everything frictionlessness. Why would we not want more convenience or efficiency? The costs of our no-friction addiction, paid in our privacy and well-being, have become increasingly clear. Friction, including rules and norms, cognitive functions, or a moral compass, is necessary in so many aspects of our lives, including real relationships, collaboration, and democracy. We need to be able to tolerate boredom or discomfort to learn and to be able to discuss hard problems. Like applying brakes or changing gears on a bike, how and where to apply friction requires nuance.

---

3   Estrin, J. (June 2022) "Innovating Innovation," Medium.com. https://medium.com/@judy_estrin/out-of-whack-3aab64d28625

4   Estrin, J. (Sept 2018) "Authoritarian Technology: Attention!" Medium.com https://medium.com/@judy_estrin/authoritarian-technology-attention-e4c34585d114

5   Estrin, J. (Sept 2024) "Stop Drinking From the Toilet!" .Coda. https://www.codastory.com/authoritarian-tech/stop-drinking-from-the-toilet/

After years under the rule of authoritarian technology we are now more reactive, reductionist, and fragmented, our worlds gamified around financial rewards. All-or-nothing extreme thinking has torn our social fabric, conditioning many to endorse an authoritarian path and others to opt out completely. This is now far more than a tech problem. Through narrative, political, and research capture, the Silicon Valley way is now echoed throughout society—evidenced by what we see today in D.C.

Redefining our model of leadership in the private and public sectors is critical to our future. This will require reaffirming our values; embracing decision-making approaches that are both reactive and proactive, competitive and collaborative; creating aspirational narratives that can unite; and reforming the incentives that are tearing us apart.

Imagine a culture that values dignity and consideration[6]—not dominance and extremism. Sustainable innovation is driven by a balance of questioning, openness, risk, patience, and trust—the core values that together enable a capacity for change. Picture the encouragement of social cohesion, balancing rights *and* responsibilities, embracing curiosity and agility instead of false expectation and promise of certainty. Envision that we accept friction as a vital function—especially in confronting our internal contradictions. We must be able to simultaneously hold two truths and conflicting feelings, not flee to whatever offers (often a false sense of) clarity and comfort.

In the words of Einstein, "We cannot solve our problems with the same thinking we used to create them." Our leadership-centric culture has fundamentally broken down, yet fully decentralized approaches don't work at large scale. We need to address how we solve problems, from the halls of power to the playground. The parable of the blindfolded men and

---

6   Grant, A. (April 2025) "America Is Learning the Wrong Lesson From Elon Musk," *The New York Times.* https://www.nytimes.com/2025/04/13/opinion/elon-musk-leadership-business-education.html

the elephant perfectly captures our current problem-solving approach—not just because the majestic elephant is so overwhelming that we focus on what we can see and do now. As the story goes, everyone insists that their part is the complete picture—they are *the* leader.

Enduring strength goes beyond the glitter of charisma to the soundness that comes from well-considered and articulated values, vision, and decision-making processes. To both attract followers and deliver for them, we need to move beyond a singular focus on individual personalities of leader*ship*, to leader*hood*—leadership systems with and for each other. In a leaderhood system each of us has the capacity to lead and be led, to teach, and to learn. There is a focus on responsibility, not just authority, and building relationship trust, not blind faith. This requires real conversation, not just social media fights, among those who have power of position, power of ideas, and power of numbers. In order to move fast and *not* break things we need more elasticity in how we make decisions. Too often decision making follows either "only I can fix it" or "wisdom of the crowds" extremes. With a capacity for discretion, critical thinking, and robust information flow, nuance can be applied.

In our *"now culture,"* anything that does not give us immediate gratification or contribute to the bottom line is not valued. Proactive and connective efforts are some of the critical roles many of our institutions play, in government, academia, civil society, and journalism. They are too often viewed as overhead or irrelevant. These organizations' leaders need to lead—not entrench themselves in defending the status quo. We must acknowledge where we are not delivering and demonstrate a capacity for change. Tearing institutions down is not the answer—we need to add and adapt, not subtract, to remodel around purpose and values.

Let's apply our creativity to new narratives that reflect our values *and* get sustained engagement, not just transient spikes of attention. Meet the moment with an inspirational, yet realistic, vision of a future that people will aspire to *and* believe we can deliver on—not more magical/utopian thinking. When we try to homogenize and simplify the complexity that makes us human we fail to connect with individuals—we need more

AND not more ISM. While not losing our ideals, we can change our tone and focus on structural accountability over transient shaming. We must resist the overriding influence of the algorithms, for it is clear that we cannot force change by yelling louder, fueling the fires of those who want to tear down without any idea of how to rebuild.

We must transform the financial and social incentives that fuel today's zero-sum norms, which homogenize and reduce humans to collections of data points. It's time to replace growth for growth's sake with growth for meaning's sake. A more distributed approach to growth, modeled after the original Internet infrastructure, is what I call *interconnecting diversity*. In this model, businesses, organizations, or communities—each with their own different rules for how they are operated and governed, who they serve, and how they are led—are interconnected at a foundational level with shared information flow, mission, and values. We should celebrate businesses solving real problems and bringing value to society—not just valuations. We should incentivize new investment and mentoring vehicles to support great businesses that may not fit into the VC search for unicorns. We can inspire fresh approaches through testing and experimentation in "greenhouse" environments. For any of this to work, we must address the erosion of critical thinking in adults and our youth.

I interviewed more than 100 leaders for my book, including Vint Cerf, Marc Andreessen, Andy Grove, Reed Hastings, and Reid Hoffman. Leaders with a breadth of political views, but we all believed in scientific discovery and technological innovation over absolute certainty. Authoritarians fuel feelings of chaos and fear to reinforce their power. I challenge us to develop a culture to replace utopian thinking with curiosity—diminish absolutism and encourage trust with questioning and autonomy with reflection. That begins with those of us who have the luxury of the time and resources to think about change.

We cannot confront today's challenges if each of us claim that our piece solves *the* problem. We need to keep sight of the whole elephant and integrate multiple perspectives, not look for singular, immediate answers. As leaders, we must demonstrate rather than dictate—reduce extremism in both content and tone and listen and integrate before we rush to persuade. If we relinquish our quest for dominance, and disrupt with consideration and dignity, we can accept the necessary friction—and in turn—move at the right speed and build. ★

The Future of an American Education

We must confront the challenges of new technologies, socioeconomic disparities, and ideological influences on the curriculum to produce a well-informed citizenry.

BY MICHAEL J. SORRELL, ED.D.

President, Paul Quinn College

The average American is being underserved by our nation's educational system. Too many students do not possess a basic understanding of their own history or government.[1] Many children sit in uninspiring classrooms, taught by overwhelmed and underpaid teachers.[2] Our colleges and universities, once the gateway to hope and financial security, now saddle too many generations of families with insurmountable debt.[3]

---

1   American Council of Trustees and Alumni. *ACTA Releases Alarming New Survey Showing Dangerous Level of Civic Illiteracy Among College Students.* July 2024. https://www.goacta.org/2024/07/acta-releases-alarming-new-survey-showing-dangerous-level-of-civic-illiteracy-among-college-students/

2   Steiner, Elizabeth D., and Ashley Woo. *Teachers' Well-Being and Intentions to Leave: Results from the 2023 State of the American Teacher Survey.* RAND Corporation, 2023. https://www.rand.org/pubs/research_reports/RRA1108-12.html

3   Consumer Financial Protection Bureau. Insights from the 2023–24 Student Loan Borrower Survey. 2024. https://www.consumerfinance.gov/data-research/research-reports/insights-from-the-2023-2024-student-loan-borrower-survey/

Combined with a cost of living that requires entire households to work multiple jobs to make ends meet, it becomes clear that the next iteration of America holds no promise of matching the prosperity of the generations that preceded it. This reality has left Americans angry, desperate, and willing to look backwards for answers. Backwards to a time they have been deceived into believing was better for people like them. Backwards to a time that can only be achieved by sacrificing the very tenets of our democracy and the dreams of fellow countrymen.

It is in this pivotal moment that I propose a new vision—not only for the American educational system, but for the future of America itself. This vision is rooted in pragmatism and propelled by ambition. It acknowledges the everyday challenges facing American families while addressing the urgent need to educate and engage all citizens. From the growing threat to our democracy to the profound disruptions posed by artificial intelligence, we must confront the forces reshaping our world with clarity, courage, and a renewed commitment to an informed, empowered public.

In reimagining the future of the American educational system and its students, we must begin by acknowledging a basic truth: The American educational system finds itself at a crossroads unlike any it has faced before. Never in our history have so many direct beneficiaries of an American education been so deeply invested in destroying the system that created their success. This reality is compounded by the embrace of disinformation and the whitewashing of history. Lastly, while we have experienced technological advances before, we have never seen anything with the potential to alter every facet of the learning process like artificial intelligence. This combination of forces leads us into the eye of the perfect educational storm, where the basic premise of education is not only being challenged but, in many cases, discredited and divested from.

To build a modern educational system that serves the average American as well as it does the affluent, it is necessary to begin at the foundation. The first question we must ask strikes at the core of learning: What is school? Once we have established what we would like our schools to look like for the next 10 to 15 years (a realistic period given the pace of societal and technological change), we can move to our second design question: Who decides what our students will learn? Finally, and perhaps the most critical, we must determine the role we want technology, more specifically AI, to play in our classrooms. While the answers to these questions will not solve all our dilemmas, they will allow us to begin crafting a model that will return hope and greater expectations to the classrooms of our schools and universities.

★

WHAT IS SCHOOL?

The answer to this question was once simple, or so we were led to believe. Our K–12 schools were places where communities sent their children to be educated by teachers who were from the neighborhoods and knew the students and their families. Students learned material that gave them real options in life. The college-going crowd was prepared for the rigors of higher education. Everyone else was taught a trade and found a home in one of the unions and factories of our country. Such jobs ensured that these Americans could access the middle-class lives promised by the American Dream.

College, we were told, involved: 1) tenure and research-focused professors; 2) classrooms overflowing with traditional-aged students who sought a campus-based co-ed experience rooted in Greek life and sports; and 3) post-graduation jobs in abundance. No one worried about loan debt, Pell Grant recipients didn't exist, and work-readiness was assumed.

To the extent that this idyllic picture was ever real, it certainly isn't anymore. Per the National Center for Education Statistics (NCES), the average K–12 student comes from a suburban household and qualifies for free or reduced-price lunch. They are more likely to be a student of color than White, and only one in three of them will be proficient in math and reading by the eighth grade.[4] K–12 statistics such as these contribute

---

4 National Center for Education Statistics, *The Nation's Report Card: 2022 NAEP Mathematics and Reading Assessments,* U.S. Department of Education, https://www. nationsreportcard.gov/

to the results that the Lumina Foundation found in their research on post-secondary students. Research from the Lumina Foundation reveals that more than a third of undergraduate students are 25 or older, approximately 80 percent are working while attending college, and 44 percent are financially independent from their parents and putting themselves through school.[5] The truth of the matter is that modern students require schools and universities that are more inclusive and reflect the reality of their lives.

Meeting this moment means embracing a dynamic model of instruction, evaluation, and promotion. We must move the expectations of success regarding our students from possible to probable and then, to inevitable. To do that, we must first draw a more meaningful connection for our K–12 schools to higher education and industry. One way of accomplishing this is to create a seamless relationship between K–12 school districts and the colleges and universities in their region. I believe that post-secondary institutions should guarantee college acceptance to every middle school student in their neighboring school districts that meets their admissions criteria. By doing this, American children see higher education as an opportunity for all those with the desire, as opposed to a place only for the privileged.

On the industry side, our high schools should create tracks that guarantee meaningful employment in high-demand, underserved sectors within their communities. For example, I have yet to encounter a hospital or medical center that does not have a shortage of nurses and physician's assistants.[6] America will be short 550,000 plumbers by 2027[7] and employment of electricians is expected to grow twice as fast as the average for all

5   Lumina Foundation, *Today's Student,* https://www.luminafoundation.org/campaign/todays-student/

6   American Association of Colleges of Nursing, *Nursing Shortage Fact Sheet,* n.d., https://www.aacnnursing.org/news-data/fact-sheets/nursing-shortage

7   Fionna Mao, "America's Plumber Deficit Isn't Good for the Economy," *Bloomberg,* March 14, 2024, https://www.bloomberg.com/news/articles/2024-03-14/plumber-jobs-have-high-demand-in-us-with-competitive-salary

other occupations through 2032.[8] These are well-paid jobs that will provide financial stability without a four-year degree. It does not undercut our college-going culture or focus to simply address areas of obvious need.

At the college level, it is long past time for our industry to adopt competency-based education that allows students to earn credit when they demonstrate subject mastery, not finish a minimum number of attendance hours. Colleges and universities must also do away with the idea that majors are the only credential graduates should leave campus with. At Paul Quinn College, we have rejected the "diploma only" model in favor of giving students multiple ways of earning post-graduation opportunities. Our program is called the "Four Pillars."

The Four Pillars are:
1. Subject Matter Mastery (your major);
2. Experiential Learning (off-campus internships for pay);
3. PQCx (industry-recognized certificates); and
4. Every Quinnite Is an Entrepreneur (all PQC students must create a business prior to their graduation).

The problem with our educational model isn't that it was never adequate. On the contrary. The American educational model was good. The problem is that we stayed wedded to the model for far too long. Our students and our society have outgrown it. Education should meet people where they are and expand their ability to dream. Changing how we define school will allow us to do that.

---

8 U.S. Bureau of Labor Statistics, "Electricians," *Occupational Outlook Handbook,* April 17, 2024, https://www.bls.gov/ooh/construction-and-extraction/electricians.htm

★

WHO CONTROLS THE CURRICULUM?

Carter G. Woodson once wrote that "[i]f you can control a man's thinking, you do not have to worry about his actions."[9] In too many of our states, educators and students spend their time preoccupied with preparing for state-mandated standardized tests. In theory, the tests measure student learning outcomes.[10] In reality, however, the tests measure how well schools have prepared their students for the test. Given the high stakes involved—student performance influences everything from funding to staff retention—there is great incentive for schools to prioritize teaching to the test over actual learning.

The problem with teaching to standardized tests is that doing so does not leave space for students to learn how to think. Instead, this approach rewards rote memorization, mastering test-taking methods over critical thinking, and demands fidelity to a narrow group of subjects. The result of this methodology is students who are left ill-equipped and uninspired.

To combat this problem, we must prioritize returning the ability to think into our classrooms. This feat can be achieved by constructing a classroom experience that cultivates entrepreneurial thought and action by introducing Reality-Based Education into every level of our educational system. Reality-Based Education focuses on pragmatic problem-solving and offers real-time assessment in ways that do not exist at scale today. Imagine an educational experience that adjusts for grade level and allows all students to engage intellectually in devising remedies for the challenges of the day (climate crisis, meaningful solutions to the gun violence epidemic, etc.); learn the fundamentals of engineering and

---

9 Carter G. Woodson, *The Mis-Education of the Negro* (Washington, D.C.: Associated Publishers, 1933).

10 Education Writers Association, "Testing and Test Prep: How Much Is Too Much?," n.d., https://ewa.org/news-explainers/testing-and-test-prep-how-much-is-too-much

architecture by redesigning their communities; and master history, economic development, ethics, and international politics. Such classroom experiences would inspire not only students, but also educators.

Reality-Based Education has another advantage that makes it appealing in this moment—it can be a step forward in depoliticizing education and curriculum design. Ten years ago, I never questioned facts. Truthfully, I still do not. What I do question are those individuals who ask us to believe that history should be edited for their comfort or to fit a narrow political agenda. We are living in a period where historical revisionism has infected our schools and communities. In far too many places, history is being perverted in the interest of emotional comfort or political gain. This is wrong and threatens to radicalize what should be a safe space—the classrooms of our country.

The average school board and elected state officials are not qualified to dictate what students should be taught. In giving them this power, we open the door to intellectual corruption and manipulation. I strongly disagree with those individuals who believe facts are fluid. Facts are immutable. While context does influence our interpretation and understanding of the facts, context does not grant us permission to rewrite foundational aspects of the past.

History should not be molded by angry or biased parents at the local level, or re-election-minded officials at the state and federal levels. To control for this type of self-interest, I propose the creation of a nonpartisan, national committee of true subject-matter experts who are tasked with developing the curriculum of subjects (civics, history, math, science, computer science/AI, and English) that are deemed of national importance. This committee would be appointed by a bipartisan group of elected officials from the states whose K–12 schools are the highest performing. Recognizing that there are unique aspects to each region of our country, I propose that we allow the curricula in foreign languages and the arts to be designed by bipartisan state and local designees. By giving local committees voice in the educational process, we can craft region-specific educational opportunities that will lead to addressing the gap in employment opportunities and provide them an avenue to have their views included.

For this aspect of my vision to succeed, we must acknowledge—and learn from—the mistakes of the Common Core movement. Launched in 2009, the Common Core was one of the most ambitious education reform efforts in U.S. history.[11] Its goal was straightforward, if controversial: to create consistent and rigorous academic standards that would prevent so many American children from falling behind their global peers.[12]

While my proposal does call to mind the original Common Core, it differs in several material ways. First, what I am suggesting is far more comprehensive than the Common Core. The Common Core focused only on math and English.[13] In contrast, I am proposing a national curriculum that includes six subjects and speaks to the need to place the equal emphasis on learning history and understanding democracy as it does math. By doing so, we can avoid many of the shortcomings that have prevented the success of previous efforts and reverse the steady decline of our students when measured in the global context.[14]

Secondly, by engaging a more comprehensive committee in the design phase, I hope to build a broader, less partisan support base for the project. This will help shield the effort from the type of criticism that engulfed the Common Core until the program can gain traction. Lastly, I am fully aware of the hurdles that this recommendation must overcome in this political climate. Proposing a national curriculum flies in the face

---

11 Dana Goldstein, "What Happened to the Common Core?," *New York Times,* December 6, 2019, https://www.nytimes.com/2019/12/06/us/common-core.html

12 Ibid.

13 National Governors Association Center for Best Practices & Council of Chief State School Officers, *Common Core State Standards for English Language Arts & Literacy in History/Social Studies, Science, and Technical Subjects* (Washington, DC: Authors, 2010), https://learning.ccsso.org/wp-content/uploads/2022/11/ELA_Standards1.pdf

14 Marc Tucker, "Why Other Countries Keep Outperforming Us in Education—and How to Catch Up," *Education Week,* May 13, 2021, https://www.edweek.org/policy-politics/opinion-why-other-countries-keep-outperforming-us-in-education-and-how-to-catch-up/2021/05

of the "states' rights" school of thought. However, the degree of difficulty is no reason to forgo pursuing a worthy attempt at raising the intellectual bar of our country and reversing our nation's flirtation with anti-democratic principles.

★

WHAT DO WE DO WITH AI?

It has been 75 years since Alan Turing began research into artificial intelligence.[15] For the majority of that time, AI existed more in science fiction movies and books than in daily life. However, with the advent of OpenAI, the modern era of this technology has announced itself as here to stay. While AI is transforming many aspects of our lives, perhaps no field stands to be impacted more than education.

It is indisputable that AI will bring about much positive change in education. For example, it is not difficult to look at the self-paced learning programs and understand their value. These programs have the potential to create classroom environments that allow teachers to build lesson plans that cater to the gifted and the developing who are housed in the same spaces. Tailoring lesson plans to fit the individual needs of each learner should improve student performance.

Another advantage to utilizing AI in schools is the enhanced efficiency. Through tools like ChatGPT and Google, students have at their fingertips the ability to teach themselves much of the material that historically could only come from their instructors. Students also can access summaries of material that once took hours to do manually. It is hard to argue that such a development does not benefit students who have the access and ability to harness the power of this technology.

While the advantages of AI are seductive, one cannot help but wonder if fully embracing this technology without the proper guardrails in

---

15 A. M. Turing, "Computing Machinery and Intelligence," *Mind* 59, no. 236 (1950): 433–460.

place will not ultimately become a Faustian bargain. For example, the claims that using self-paced learning AI software in the classroom will be a boon to those schools dealing with overcrowding ignores a critical fact.[16] The schools most impacted by overcrowding are in communities more likely to be grappling with the digital divide. Adding AI to a community without broadband or adequate computers does not improve the academic experience. Instead, it will serve as another reminder of the day-to-day inequalities these families already face.

Another example of potential issues with AI in schools is plagiarism (or "AI-giarism").[17] As students increasingly use versions of AI that are sophisticated enough to produce well-written papers and more, the debate over what qualifies as original work product has become more complex. At Paul Quinn, we experienced a situation in the last year where the unassisted work of one of our students was falsely flagged for the suspicion of using AI-generated material. The student maintained their innocence and appealed the matter to my office. In meeting with the interested parties, it became apparent to me that our institutional policies were badly out of date and underdeveloped. This episode left such an impression on me that I will be spending part of my summer enrolled in a course on AI at the University of Pennsylvania to better understand the magnitude of what we are dealing with in this area.

The final challenge with embarking upon the AI-generated path without appropriate guidance is the long-term negative impact an overreliance on technology has on students.[18] Researchers have discovered that excess use of technology by students in and outside of the classroom leads to undesirable outcomes in the areas of student psychological,

---

16 Y. Wang and X. Li, "Artificial Intelligence Ecosystem for Automating Self-Directed Teaching," *arXiv* preprint, November 2024, https://arxiv.org/pdf/2411.07300.pdf

17 J. Chan, "Is AI Changing the Rules of Academic Misconduct? An In-Depth Look at Students' Perceptions of 'AI-giarism'," *arXiv preprint*, June 2023, https://arxiv.org/pdf/2306.03358.pdf

18 M. Anderson, "Negative Effects of Technology: Psychological, Social, and Physical," *Medical News Today,* March 14, 2024, https://www.medicalnewstoday.com/articles/negative-effects-of-technology

physical, and mental health.[19] Additionally, it has also been proven that heavy reliance on technology harms students' ability to think critically.[20]

I am not proposing a future where AI does not exist in our schools. There is too much potential in the tool to leave it out of the conversation. Rather, I am an advocate for a more reasoned and thoughtful approach than what we are doing now. The answer for our future is not "either/or," but "both/and."

CONCLUSION

It is hard to look at the state of America and not lay a portion of the blame at the feet of our educational system. The people primarily benefitting from the attacks on democracy and our rule of law, racism, and misogyny were all educated in American schools. While that divisiveness may not have been learned in class, our educational system did not do enough to quash it. This is a problem that must be addressed moving forward.

But what does addressing this problem look like? I believe that when done right, schools should produce students who see themselves as key actors in their own educations. In such an environment, students are problem-solvers who return to their families each night inspired by what they have learned during the day. These types of scholars develop deep pride in their schools, communities, and country. Schools, the ones our nation deserves, must be homes to diverse ideas and people who teach a variety of skills. They are places where an honest portrayal of history does not dissuade students from a love of country. On the contrary,

---

19 Jean M. Twenge, *iGen: Why Today's Super-Connected Kids Are Growing Up Less Rebellious, More Tolerant, Less Happy—and Completely Unprepared for Adulthood* (New York: Atria Books, 2017).

20 C. A. Royce and V. Bennett, "To Think or Not to Think: The Impact of AI on Critical-Thinking Skills," *NSTA Blog,* National Science Teaching Association, March 10, 2025, https://www.nsta.org/blog/think-or-not-think-impact-ai-critical-thinking-skills

teaching students the truth provides them with an appreciation for what our country has achieved.

Our schools do not have to be perfect. However, they must be places that are capable of evolving and meeting the changing environments that our students are asked to navigate daily. Our children deserve nothing less. ★

Authoritarianism Comes to America, Redux

Once we believed our democratic institutions would hold.
But today we see how quickly those institutions can
be captured and crumble, opening a path for tyranny.
The threat is not coming. It is already here.

BY SHARON DAVIES

President and CEO of the Charles F. Kettering Foundation

Americans are living through a time of great threat to our democracy—not from an external power, but from our own president. Examples of this threat abound and can be quickly summarized. They include: the executive branch's dismissive attitude toward the rule of law, encroachments on the rights and liberties of persons, a weakening of our system of checks and balances and separation of power principles, the utilization of the Department of Justice and the FBI as weapons against the president's critics, threats against a free press, assaults on the academic freedom of our nation's colleges and universities, efforts to undermine the impartial administration of elections, efforts to sow rather than heal divisions among the populace, and attacks on truth and fact.

Not for the first time democracy scholars have worried that a Donald Trump presidency might topple our democratic experiment.

During his first term, a group contributed essays to a volume edited by law professor Cass R. Sunstein, *Can It Happen Here? Authoritarianism in America[1]*. In one of those essays,[2] Eric Posner concluded that Trump would have to take an everything-everywhere-all-at-once approach to become anything more than an *aspiring* dictator, which struck him at the time as unlikely. Without such a multi-front approach, Posner thought, Trump would likely be stopped by the bevy of democratic institutions our founders wisely erected precisely to prevent despotic rule.

That is, the president would have to simultaneously: attack the press; silence Congress; use the FBI, CIA, and IRS to harass his opponents; replace disloyal civil servants with loyalists; co-opt the military; subdue the judiciary; impose his will on state and local governments; bend the Republican Party to his will; attack civil society; and create a mob willing to do his bidding, Posner wrote. Coordinating all those moves seemed unlikely, he thought, and even if attempted they would only succeed *if all those democratic institutions failed to "rely on one another for support."*[3]

One hundred days into Trump's second term, Posner's prescient list looks like a running rollcall of Trump's recent executive orders. Check, check, check, check. It thus bears considering Posner's warning about the importance of mutual support. He wrote that "the institutions that may block an aspiring dictator depend on one another for mutual support."[4] If that mutual support crumbles, a far less democratic future for Americans becomes imaginable.

A free press can resist a dictator through courageous reporting, Posner explained, but maybe they won't if the judiciary has been infiltrated or if judges have been intimidated to relax the First Amendment's protection of journalists—or if disfavored reporters and news outlets are

---

1   *Can It Happen Here? Authoritarianism in America,* ed. Cass A. Sunstein (HarperCollins, New York, NY 2018).

2   Eric A. Posner, *The Dictator's Handbook, U.S. Edition,* 1-10 in *Ibid.*

3   *Ibid,* 3-16

4   *Ibid,* 16-17

labeled propagandists and deprived funding (or worse). Judges can block illegal orders, he wrote, but maybe they won't if they are threatened with impeachment or fear the prospect of their orders going unenforced. Congress can stand up against a despot, but maybe they won't if they fear their constituents will vote them out of office if they do or threaten them and their families with violence. "Thus, while a frontal assault by the would-be dictator on a single institution standing alone seems bound to fail, it is possible that a series of more modest actions on multiple fronts, executed patiently over a long period of time, could eventually produce dictatorial power," Posner warned.

As president and CEO of the Kettering Foundation, I have found myself talking frequently about the need for mutual alliance to have any hope of defeating the anti-democratic aims of our current president. Citizens are more powerful than they think, but it is their numbers that make them a force with which to reckon.

I thus write here with several aims. First, to give simple witness to the campaign of threats the Trump administration is waging against civil society and our democratic system of governance in his quest for uncabined power. Authoritarians seek to erase history that is inconvenient to their preferred narratives; we must act to record and preserve it. Second, to echo Posner's warning about the need for mutual alliance to meet the threat that this administration presents to our democracy. Third, to act with courage, as one example among many, in the hope that others will do the same.

BEARING WITNESS

In an era of contested truth and fact, it has become important to document the attacks the president has unleashed on civil society just months into his second term. Such "record making" may also help overcome the tendency of Americans to underestimate the magnitude of the threat that the Trump administration poses to our democracy.

Since the return of Donald Trump to the White House, governing by threat has become the administration's most apparent *modus operandi*. He has threatened the nation's top universities with lawsuits, investigations, the loss of federal funding, and the revocation of their tax-exempt status.

He has threatened elite law firms with the revocation of security clearances and access to federal buildings, such as courthouses, while coercing from them promises of *pro bono* work aligned with the administration's goals.

He has threatened news outlets with time-consuming and expensive lawsuits, excluded reporters from access to the White House when they refuse to parrot his view of the world, and labeled public television and radio as fonts of propaganda and threatened their federal funding.

He has declared all diversity, equity, and inclusion practices "illegal racial discrimination" without a single judicial finding to that effect and ordered the disbandment of DEI offices in public and private workplaces, resulting in the loss of countless jobs.

He has threatened major foundations with investigations and empowered the Secretary of the Treasury to designate charitable organizations as supporters of foreign terrorist organizations without a burden of proof.

He has trampled on rules against firing individuals performing independent watchdog roles and reversed the focus of the Office of Civil Rights at DOJ, leaving complainants with credible voter suppression claims without a government advocate.

He has unleashed a torrent of state and federal actions that threaten and punish transgender people simply for existing, including an executive order restricting access to gender-affirming care and banning transgender Americans from military service, and has rolled back protections for members of the LGBTQ+ community more broadly.

All that and much more within 100 days of retaking the White House, then tweeting he is "just getting started."

★

COLLECTIVE DEFENSE IS REQUIRED

The implicit message being sent to the American public through these aggressions is unmistakable: Resistance is futile. If the nation's most powerful firms and robustly endowed institutions can be intimidated into silence or compliance, what possible good can come from resistance by far less powerful organizations and everyday citizens?

But that is exactly wrong. As we have seen, universities and law firms acting alone to negotiate terms with this administration have been no match for its aims. As Posner suggested, mutual defense will be key, and success lies in understanding our own collective power.

Happily, there are signs that a wave of resistance has begun to sweep the nation. Despite the Trump administration's repressive campaign, not all have been muzzled, and each act of defiance has seemed to embolden others. Georgetown University pushed back against a threatening governmental letter about what it can teach its students. The president of Princeton University vowed to fight as well, as did Harvard University, under pressure from its faculty. In a powerful show of collective resolve, the Association for American Colleges and Universities issued "A Call for Constructive Engagement"[5] signed by more than 600 college and university leaders, rejecting the administration's political interference in the role of higher education in a democratic society.

The law firms Perkins Coie, Wilmer Cutler, Willams and Connolly, Jenner & Block, the Elias Law Group, and others have pressed forward despite threats that have paralyzed some of their peers. The Article III Coalition, a bipartisan coalition of former federal judges, released a letter in defense of the independence of the judiciary and the constitutional role of the courts. Civil society organizations like the ACLU and Democracy

---

5   "A Call for Constructive Engagement," (April 2025) AACU.org. https://www.aacu.org/newsroom/a-call-for-constructive-engagement

Forward and state attorneys general have filed lawsuit after lawsuit, frustrating the administration's so-called "100 days of thunder."

Citizens are also embracing the responsibilities of engagement in a democratic society. Everyday Americans have boycotted multibillion-dollar corporations for giving up their DEI commitments without a fight. Electric car buyers have shunned Tesla in protest of the actions of CEO Elon Musk. Community organizers have led rallies and marches and silent vigils, delivering a clear message: *Hands Off.* When the president told the governor of Maine that her state "had better comply" with his executive order banning transgender athletes from participating in sports aligning with their gender identities, she replied flatly, "We'll see you in court."

These acts of resistance have shown that capitulating to the government is one choice. Standing up against it is another.

In times of great threat to things of great value, each will be called to take a stand. There are no free passes, and history will judge where we stood.

★

MOVING FROM FEAR INTO COURAGE

Fearlessness is not required to act in defense of democracy, but courage may be. Although the two are sometimes confused, acting courageously is not the same thing as being fearless. Fear is a natural response to real and perceived threats. Courage is summoning the willingness to act despite one's fear.

This is a particularly important distinction to keep in mind when one's own government is the source of that fear. American freedoms are constitutionally protected, but courage has always been required when government actors have used their power to repress them, whether by firehose, billy club, or German Shepherds. It is rational to fear such things. It is no less rational to worry about the costs to one's organization (and the individuals and families that constitute and depend on them) from a vindictive president bent on unconstrained power.

But it is past time for civil society to let go of the hope that "becoming small" or attempting to "ride things out" will be enough to save us. Failing to grasp the magnitude of the threat that this administration presents will cause us to move too gingerly, at the cost of our democracy.

Therefore, I contribute this essay to this anthology as one act of open defiance, to join arms with those who have stood up before me. I denounce the executive branch's abuse of its powers against a free society. And for the sake of our democracy, I pray that others will find their own ways to do the same. ★

★

New Perspectives

Each wave of new Americans presents an opportunity to see why the democratic experiment matters so much. Even when America has failed to live up to its promise, we have remained a beacon of hope to the world.

The Promise of Universal Opportunity

The American Dream was never about
guaranteeing identical outcomes for everyone,
but it must provide equal opportunities for everyone
to pursue their own version of success.

BY MARI MANOOGIAN
Executive director, The Next 50

When I was first elected to the Michigan House of Representatives in 2018, I was 26 years old—the youngest woman serving in the legislature at that time. My path to politics and public service wasn't predestined. I'm the great-granddaughter of Armenian Genocide survivors who fled to America and settled in Detroit in the early twentieth century. My family arrived at Ellis Island with almost nothing, they didn't speak English, and they were still reliving the trauma of the genocide. Even still, they believed in the promise of this country: that with hard work, determination, and access to opportunity, you could rebuild and hope the generations that follow are better off than the last.

This belief in opportunity—this faith in America's promise—is what has kept me going during this time of uncertainty and instability. In a time of growing cynicism and division, the concept of American Universalism offers a framework built on three pillars: universal opportunity, universal freedom, and universal rights. It's a vision that unites rather than divides— one that speaks to our highest aspirations as a nation while addressing the urgent challenges we face.

★

UNIVERSAL OPPORTUNITY: THE FOUNDATION OF THE AMERICAN PROMISE

The American Dream isn't about promising identical outcomes for all; it's about ensuring universal opportunity—the chance for everyone to pursue their own version of success and fulfillment. When that opportunity is genuinely accessible to all, not just the privileged few, we create the conditions for a stronger, more secure nation.

Growing up in Michigan, I was raised on stories of what my family lost in the genocide, but also what they built here in America. My great-grandparents arrived with almost nothing, yet were able to start businesses, purchase homes, and see their children receive an education they themselves could only dream of. They worked incredibly hard, but they also benefited from systems that rewarded that hard work: public schools that educated students of all backgrounds, an economy that placed a high value on merit, and communities that, eventually, accepted them as neighbors and fellow Americans, as they balanced their identity as Americans of Armenian heritage.

Today those foundational elements of opportunity are crumbling, if non-existent, for too many Americans. Too many of us, including those in power today, are more interested in fanning the flames of tribalism and encouraging zero-sum thinking, which will only hold us back as a nation. We face a choice as a nation: we can continue to divide and pit neighbors against neighbors and abandon our core principals as Americans, or we can rebuild the infrastructure of opportunity in a way that works for everyone and reclaim the American Dream.

★

LESSONS FROM HISTORY

I'm under no illusion that my family's story is somehow unique. In fact, our story of survival and rebirth is as American as apple pie. Millions have come to these shores fleeing persecution, violence, and despair. My great-grandparents survived a systematic attempt to erase an entire people from existence by a government that used tribalism to pit neighbor against neighbor in the worst possible way. The trauma of living through the horror of the Armenian Genocide shaped generations of my family, but so did America's promise of renewal.

What allowed my family to rebuild was not special treatment. It was, along with hard work and some advocacy, access to universal opportunities that should be available to every American: good schools, fair wages, safe communities, and a government that chooses sanity over chaos. It was the ability to work hard and see that work rewarded. It was becoming part of a society where merit and effort matter more than background or birthplace.

The lesson of my family's journey is not just about perseverance; it's about what kind of country makes such renewal possible. A country that, despite its imperfections, strives to create systems and structures that give everyone a fair shot.

I'm not blind to the ways America has fallen short of its ideals. I acknowledge that opportunity has never been applied equally, and that the early foundations of our nation's economic system were laid with slave labor. In this century, rather than abandoning the promise of universal opportunity, we must fight to fulfill it. This work must be grounded in the lived experiences of Americans across every region, demographic, and background—which is why I believe in the vision of American Universalism, a vision that intentionally bridges generational, geographic, and ideological divides.

What we need is a new infrastructure for the twenty-first century—one that accounts for the changing nature of work, the climate crisis, technological disruption, and the unique challenges facing younger generations. The most effective response to authoritarianism and division isn't just resistance—it's building something better.

★

UNIVERSAL FREEDOM AND RIGHTS: THE GUARDRAILS OF OPPORTUNITY

While opportunity forms the foundation of the American universalism vision, I recognize that opportunity cannot thrive without freedom and rights. These three pillars are inseparable.

My ancestors fled to America not just for economic opportunity, but for freedom—freedom from persecution, freedom to worship, freedom to speak their language and practice their culture. They sought a place where their basic humanity would be recognized through equal rights under law.

Universal freedom means that all Americans deserve to live without fear of oppression or violence, to make their own choices about their lives and bodies, to speak and think freely, and to pursue happiness according to their own definition. American Universalism rejects the false choice between personal liberty and collective welfare. True freedom requires both the absence of coercion and the presence of meaningful choices.

As threats to both freedom and rights intensify—from restrictions on voting to attempts to control people's bodies and private decisions—I stand firm in defense of these foundational American principles. Economic opportunity cannot be separated from civic freedom and basic rights. All three must advance together for any of them to be meaningful.

★

A NEW GENERATION'S CALL TO ACTION

As a Millennial who came of age during the Great Recession, entered politics during a time of deep polarization, and served through a global pandemic—including when an armed unruly mob, some carrying firearms, stood outside the Michigan House chamber threatening law-makers—I've witnessed how the erosion of opportunity threatens our democracy itself. When people don't believe they can build a better life through honest work and determination, they lose faith in the American project altogether.

My generation has been labeled cynical, but I see things a little differently. I see young people hungry for leadership that matches this moment's urgency, that focuses on delivering tangible improvements to people's lives, and that offers an authentic vision for a renewed American Dream—one that is affordable and accessible to the American people. And, my generation is stepping up to lead. Through my work at The Next 50, I have met hundreds of young people who are taking up the mantle of leadership and delivering for their communities.

That's why I'm drawn to American Universalism, not just as a philosophical framework but as a practical political strategy for this perilous moment. By uniting Americans around our shared desire for economic security, dignity, and the chance to build something better for our children, we can break through the toxic polarization and rebuild a society in which starting from nothing—as my family once did—doesn't determine your destiny.

The strongest movements in American history have always paired moral clarity with practical vision. They've appealed to our highest ideals while addressing immediate material needs. They've demanded that America live up to its promise for all people.

That's the kind of movement we need to build for the next 50 years. A movement that honors the journeys that brought us all here—whether our families came seeking opportunity, were brought against their will, or have been here since time immemorial—while focusing relentlessly on building systems that give everyone the chance to write their own American story.

The American Dream isn't dead—it's waiting to be renewed and expanded for the next 50 years and beyond. With universal opportunity as a foundation, and universal freedom and rights as our guardrails, we can create the conditions for millions of Americans to attain the American Dream—just as my family once did. That's the work ahead of us. Let's get started. ★

Democracy Must Be Cultivated Early On

Those who immigrate to our country have a perspective that we would all do well to remember: Freedom requires vigilance, voting matters, and democracy works best when we all participate.

BY LUIS LOZADA

CEO of Democracy Works

When my mother and her siblings fled the Dominican Republic in 1965 during a coup d'etat, she left behind a world where opportunities were limited and dissent was dangerous. For her, becoming an American citizen in 1979 wasn't just about securing a legal status—it was about embracing the ideals of a nation where the rule of law protected fundamental freedoms. I was born in 1980, and despite growing up in a single-parent home where Spanish was our primary language, I learned the value of civic engagement early on.

One of my earliest political memories is of my mother proudly wearing a presidential campaign pin during the 1988 election. As someone who had only known Ronald Reagan as president, watching my mother engage in the election taught me that choosing our leaders was something worth paying attention to. That year, I paid attention to the political ads, the vice-presidential candidates, and the debates. I learned about the stakes of elections—local, state, and federal—and the importance of being informed on potential outcomes.

My mother's reverence for America's democratic system shaped my worldview. She understood what many natural-born citizens take for granted: Democracy requires participation to thrive. For her, voting wasn't merely a right but a privilege. Even during the Covid-19 pandemic, despite being immunocompromised, she cast her ballot in person. We turned voting into a family tradition—celebrating our right to make our voices heard as well as the democratic ideals that had given us so much opportunity.

My early introduction to democratic participation laid the foundation for my academic and professional journey. I entered college as a political science major, fascinated by the inner workings of our government. Although I eventually graduated with a degree in information technology, my passion for civics and government remained. I attended law school, where I developed a profound appreciation for constitutional law, particularly First Amendment protections.

As a child of immigrants and a person of color, I often took positions that surprised my law school classmates. When radio host Don Imus faced backlash for his offensive comments about the Rutgers women's basketball team, I stood up in class to argue that such speech, however repugnant, was constitutionally protected. Similarly, when standup comedians like Michael Richards or Chris Rock were criticized for jokes that used racially insensitive terms, I pointed to the protection of unpopular speech as essential to our constitutional framework.

Two Supreme Court cases particularly shaped my understanding of the First Amendment: Brandenburg v. Ohio, which addressed cross-burning by the KKK, and National Socialist Party of America v. Village of Skokie, concerning a Nazi march through a predominantly Jewish suburb of Chicago. These cases crystallized a fundamental truth: The purpose of the First Amendment is not to protect popular speech.

Its primary purpose is to protect unpopular—even abhorrent—expression from government censorship.

There's a reason that the protection of speech, a free press, and the right of the people to peaceably assemble come first in our Constitution's Bill of Rights. The founders recognized that the ability to seek redress from government, to protest, and to speak freely forms the bedrock of American democracy. Without robust protections for free speech the marketplace of ideas crumbles—and with it our capacity for self-governance.

Today these constitutional principles face unprecedented challenges. Universities are punished for allowing students to organize protests on campus, individuals are removed from public spaces solely for expressing their opinions, and the press is increasingly attacked for reporting on the administration. We are witnessing how the rule of law is being subordinated to partisan interests. These developments, striking at the heart of the First Amendment, are now impacting our rights under the Fifth and Fourteenth Amendments—the constitutional pillars that guarantee due process and equal protection under the law.

My mother fled her homeland for a better life, seeking the opportunity to thrive in a country that valued and protected civil rights. The citizenship test my mother took in 1979 specifically asked her to define "the rule of law," because this principle has distinguished the U.S. from the authoritarianism she and others have experienced around the world. The promise that laws would be applied equally, regardless of status or political affiliation, represented the American ideal that inspired her journey.

As the CEO of Democracy Works, I've found a way to honor my mother's legacy while strengthening the democratic institutions she cherished. Our mission is rooted in a simple but powerful premise: Democracy functions best when participation is widespread and barriers to engagement are removed. We work tirelessly to ensure all eligible voters have the information and tools they need to participate in our democratic process.

Since our founding in 2010, our nonpartisan organization has seen how Americans increasingly rely on the Internet to gather critical information about voting in elections. Social media platforms and search engines have joined traditional news outlets as the top sources for voters seeking election information. Our goal is to meet voters where they are. In last year's national election, our organization delivered essential information to millions of voters through our partnerships across social media, search engines, AI platforms, and our voter engagement tool TurboVote. We are committed to ensuring all voters can find accurate information about when, where, and how to vote.

The challenges facing our democracy today are significant. Misinformation threatens to undermine public trust, while polarization strains our civic fabric. Yet I remain optimistic because I believe most Americans understand the value of our democracy. When individual voters show up at the polls—regardless of party affiliation—they affirm their commitment to self-governance and the constitutional principles that unite us.

As we approach the 250th anniversary of the Constitution, we must recommit ourselves to these foundational ideals. The Fifteenth Amendment explicitly guarantees all citizens the right to vote—a right my mother exercised faithfully after taking her oath. This connection between citizenship and voting underscores the special responsibility of being an American.

Democracy is not simply a system of government; it's a covenant between citizens and their nation. It requires vigilant protection of constitutional rights, and it demands participation, especially during times of national division. And it thrives when organizations like Democracy Works break down barriers to civic engagement.

My journey as a child of immigrants to becoming the CEO of Democracy Works reflects the promise of the American experiment. It's a testament to what's possible when constitutional principles are honored and democratic participation is encouraged. As we work to preserve the next 250 years of American democracy, I remain committed to the values my mother taught me: that freedom requires vigilance, that voting matters, and that democracy works best when we all participate. ★

The (New) American Dream

By reducing the American Dream to an accumulation of wealth, we have diminished our capacity to flourish as humans. A reimagining of the dream would instead draw its strength from the increasing diversity that defines our nation.

BY PHILIPPA PHAM HUGHES

Former social practice resident at the Kennedy Center, visiting artist at the University of Michigan Museum of Art, and lecturer at the Ford School of Public Policy at the University of Michigan

I am an American.

I know I am, because my parents filed a "Report of Birth Abroad of a Citizen of the United States of America" with the U.S. Consul in the Philippines, stating that they had met all the requirements to assure my citizenship. On the same day that my parents reported my birth, the U.S. State Department issued a birth certificate and a U.S. passport.

These documents were the evidence of my American birthright, guaranteeing my right to enjoy the benefits of U.S. citizenship. To seize the American Dream. Today that dream seems to have been corrupted into a simple pursuit of wealth—at the cost of our human flourishing.

In his farewell address, Ronald Reagan said, "You can go to live in Germany or Turkey or Japan, but you cannot become a German, a Turk, or a Japanese. But anyone, from any corner of the Earth, can come to live in America and become an American." Even though I was born American, I still had to become American. My Asian face would always mark me as a foreigner. I sometimes wished I could carry my American documents with me for the times when people would ask me, where are you *really* from?

To become an American in Reagan's America meant assimilating. As a little girl I held up my eyelids and pinched the top of my nose in a futile attempt at whitening my features. I learned the Puritan work ethic from Jo March and the scrappy pioneer spirit from Laura Ingalls Wilder; in college I was even a member of the Scandinavian Interest Club. To join the American melting pot meant melting into Whiteness.

To assimilate meant sacrificing essential parts of myself. I rejected my Vietnamese heritage, suppressed my artistic inclinations, and made myself small and palatable. These compromises allowed me to achieve the material trappings typically associated with the American Dream. I never felt like I belonged, though. I never achieved my fullest potential. No matter how much material wealth I acquired, I would never be fully considered American.

My Asian face would always betray me.

As we approach America's 250th birthday this year, I envision a New American Dream—one that honors its original meaning, yet evolves beyond it. This reimagined dream transcends mere material wealth, embracing instead the full flourishing of every American. It celebrates our individual and collective ability to contain multitudes and draws strength from the increasing diversity that defines our nation.

★

THE ORIGINAL AMERICAN DREAM

James Truslow Adams coined the term "American Dream" in his 1931 book *The Epic of America*. He defined it as a dream of a land where life should be better, richer, and fuller for everyone, with opportunity for each according to ability or achievement. The core of Adams' American Dream was not about material wealth but about social equality and human dignity.

Writing during the Great Depression, Adams specifically warned that the pursuit of mere material prosperity was undermining what he saw as the true American Dream. He wasn't against economic stability—in fact, he recognized it as necessary for human dignity. What he objected to was the single-minded pursuit of wealth at the expense of other values. He worried that focusing too much on financial success would create new social barriers rather than dismantling them. His concerns have proven prophetic as wealth disparities have reached levels not seen since his era.

Adams believed this dream was unique to America because of its founding principles of equality and its historic role as a land of opportunity for immigrants seeking a better life. However, he also acknowledged that the country often fell short of fully realizing these ideals.

★

THE DREAM TODAY

Today, the American Dream is commonly understood as a path to wealth accumulation—making more money, buying bigger homes, acquiring more stuff. But this understanding has gone awry, contributing to staggering wealth disparities and disconnecting us from what Adams intended when he coined the term.

This distorted vision of endless material acquisition has established a zero-sum mentality in which success comes at someone else's expense, and human value is measured primarily through financial metrics. It has normalized levels of inequality that undermine democracy itself—concentrating not just wealth but power and opportunity in fewer and fewer hands.

We've created a moral hierarchy based on wealth that contradicts our democratic principles—valuing the voices of the affluent above others, undervaluing essential but lower-paid work, applying different standards of accountability, and allowing money to directly influence politics. The pursuit of possessions has eroded our families, communities, and personal well-being, too. Our system increasingly replaces government "of the people, by the people, for the people" with governance determined by wealth rather than citizenship.

★

THE NEW AMERICAN DREAM:
TO FLOURISH

I propose we return to Adams' original vision and update it for our contemporary context. In my vision, the New American Dream centers human flourishing.

Flourishing transcends mere success or happiness—it represents the full realization of human potential and well-being across all dimensions of life. Unlike prosperity, flourishing encompasses intellectual, emotional, physical, social, and spiritual well-being. When we flourish, we experience not just material sufficiency but a deeper sense of meaning, purpose, and connection. Only when everyone flourishes can we reach the ideals of universalism—that all people regardless of their background deserve freedom, essential rights, and dignity.

In practical terms, flourishing means developing our unique talents and abilities to their fullest. It means engaging in work that challenges and fulfills us, not merely pays well. It means building relationships characterized by mutual care and respect rather than utility. It means contributing meaningfully to the communities we inhabit. Modern psychological research supports this understanding, finding that genuine well-being comes from autonomy, competence, relatedness, and a sense of meaning—not from wealth accumulation beyond what provides for basic needs.

Collective flourishing depends on individual flourishing. Individual flourishing depends on social conditions that enable everyone to develop their capabilities. We cannot truly flourish while others are prevented from doing the same. This interconnectedness means that fostering others' flourishing ultimately enhances our own.

★

FOUR PILLARS OF
THE NEW AMERICAN DREAM

Universalism requires not just theoretical equality but the practical conditions for each person to develop their full capacities and live with dignity. To create these conditions, I propose four pillars of flourishing:

Dignity forms the cornerstone of human flourishing, recognizing the inherent and equal worth of every person regardless of their circumstances, abilities, or social position. When we honor dignity, we acknowledge that each person possesses intrinsic value simply by virtue of being human. This fundamental respect for human worth shapes how we structure our institutions, conduct our relationships, and measure success in society. Unlike achievement-based metrics of value, dignity provides a universal foundation for human rights and ethical treatment that applies equally to all. A society built on dignity rejects the notion that human value depends on productivity, wealth, status, or other external markers of "success." Instead, it creates conditions where each person can develop their unique capacities while being recognized as inherently valuable.

Belonging is fundamental to human flourishing, addressing our innate need for connection within a larger community or social fabric. When people experience genuine belonging, they are recognized and valued for their authentic selves, not merely tolerated or conditionally accepted based on their assimilation to dominant norms. This sense of being "at home" among others creates psychological safety that allows individuals to develop their unique potential without the constant anxiety of rejection or marginalization. Belonging transcends mere inclusion—it means having one's full humanity acknowledged across differences of background, appearance, or perspective. In diverse societies especially, creating conditions where everyone can belong without surrendering their distinctiveness is essential for collective flourishing. As our society becomes increasingly diverse, cultivating this deeper sense of belonging—where difference enriches rather than threatens our shared identity—becomes even more crucial to our collective flourishing.

Art and beauty are essential elements of human flourishing, serving not as mere luxuries but as vital components that nourish our fullest development. When we encounter beauty—whether in nature, visual arts, music, or literature—we experience a form of transcendence that connects us to something larger than ourselves. This connection cultivates our capacity for wonder and awe, emotions that research shows can shift us from transactional to relational ways of being. Art amplifies diverse voices, preserves cultural memory, fosters critical thinking, and creates accessible public spaces where citizens can gather across social divides. Through artistic expression, we develop empathy by imaginatively experiencing lives different from our own—a crucial capacity for a flourishing society where individuals must consider not just their personal interests but the common good. Without maintaining our capacity to recognize and create beauty, we risk losing sight of the world we seek to build and the fullness of what it means to be human.

Economic security forms the essential foundation for human flourishing. Without basic material sufficiency, the capacity for dignity is severely constrained. When people lack economic security, their focus necessarily narrows to immediate survival needs, preventing the broader development of their capacities and potential. The New American Dream rejects the notion that wealth alone creates fulfillment, while recognizing that material deprivation fundamentally restricts human possibility. Economic security is not the end goal of flourishing, but rather the necessary starting point from which authentic human flourishing can emerge. Examples of economic security include stable and living-wage employment, affordable housing, accessible healthcare, reliable transportation, adequate retirement savings, manageable debt levels, and sufficient emergency funds to weather unexpected hardships without catastrophic consequences.

Unlike the zero-sum competition embedded in conventional interpretations of the American Dream, flourishing multiplies when shared. When we create conditions for all to flourish—conditions where people can attain "the fullest stature of which they are innately capable," as Adams envisioned, we generate a positive cycle where individual and collective well-being reinforce each other.

Instead of GDP and stock market indices alone, we would value dignity, which requires seeing a person as an end in themselves, not merely as a means to economic enrichment. We would prioritize belonging, understanding that when people feel they truly belong, they can become the highest and best versions of themselves. We would emphasize art and beauty's essential roles in fostering empathy, preserving cultural memory, and building the social cohesion that democracy requires. We would recognize that basic economic security is not merely a personal achievement but a foundation for human flourishing.

★

THE AMERICAN DREAM REIMAGINED

The American Dream is not a fixed concept but one that must be continuously renegotiated to remain relevant. Just as it evolved from Adams' original vision of social equality and human dignity to the materialistic version that dominated the late twentieth century, it can and must transform again to meet the needs of today's America.

Walt Whitman declared, "The United States themselves are essentially the greatest poem." For Whitman, both poetry and democracy derive their power from creating unity amid diversity—weaving disparate voices into a harmonious whole without erasing their distinctiveness. In "I Hear America Singing," he celebrated the many kinds of individuals who make up our society: "The varied carols I hear... Each singing what belongs to him or her and to none else." This poetic vision recognizes that both individual expression and collective harmony are essential to America's promise.

In this 250th year of our nation, when we are one generation away from a majority-minority America, this vision is more vital than ever. The demographic shifts reshaping our nation aren't threats to our cohesion but opportunities to enrich our collective capacity for creativity, resilience, and innovation. When societies become more diverse but fail to be inclusive, fragmentation and polarization follow. The social fabric unravels. Democracy falters. The alternative is creating a shared narrative of belonging where different groups see themselves as part of a common future—where our unity is forged not despite our differences but because of them, each distinct voice essential to America's enduring strength and promise.

In pursuing the New American Dream, no child needs to hold up their eyelids or hide their heritage to belong. No one should have to carry documents to prove they are American enough. In this new version of the American Dream, belonging comes not from conforming but from contributing your authentic self to our collective story.

The New American Dream includes 330 million different ways to be American—330 million different American dreams. ★

Between Light and Dark: A Gen Z Case for American Universalism

The next generation of Americans must choose the Beloved Community over viral grievance.

BY HANNAH KOIZUMI AND HUGH JONES

Co-Directors of Civic Attention

★

Today's politics fuses tribalism with nihilism into a concoction so deadly that it threatens belief in the nearly 250-year-long experiment in American democracy. Across the spectrum, Americans build walls and enact rigid purity tests that decide who is welcomed as "us" and who is cast out as "them." The social media platforms where we engage with each other and consume news about what's happening in our society reward outrage, punish nuance, and shrink our sense of what this country can be; anyone who diverges from their tribe's script is cast out.

On the right, attempting to engage in frank and critical conversations about America's historical sins—and, specifically, what to do about the ways in which they still haunt us—can bring swift exile. On the left, praising the nation's achievements, celebrating the progress it has made, or voicing patriotism can do the same. One side seems to believe salvation requires glazing over America's faults and ostracizing those who seek to address them; the other suggests that the faults are fatal and patriotism itself is bigotry.

Members of Gen Z have watched this across-the-spectrum, Internet-fueled illiberalism collide with the painful reality of a government too paralyzed to solve our biggest problems. We empathize with the disillusionment of our peers, yet our own life experiences have shown us both the darkness and the light of the American story—its peril and its promise.

What the current moment demands is a recommitment to the practice of liberal patriotism: clear-eyed enough to recognize and address betrayals of our ideals, hopeful and patriotic enough to believe in and keep fighting for them. That spirit—critical, loving, and radically accepting all at once—is American Universalism.

Our personal histories and experiences have informed our passion for the America that we love and believe is still within reach.

★

HANNAH

The principles of American Universalism were inextricably woven into the stories that raised me and went on to define me. The profound sacrifices of my family during a dark period in American history, Japanese internment, act as a guiding light during this equally dark societal inflection point.

My great-grandfather and great-uncle risked their lives overseas to fight for a country that was at the same time incarcerating their loved ones back home, stripping them of all property and generational wealth. For my great-uncle Richard to receive two Purple Hearts, only to be denied membership in the Veterans of Foreign Wars because of Japanese heritage—despite generations of American citizenship—is a brutal reminder of the ways fear has been weaponized at the expense of others throughout American history.

In my family, stories of Japanese internment were never told with scorn or resentment. They were told in solemn recognition that the same nation we cherish had also wronged us in ways that were indefensible.

I have never been under the illusion that the United States is without its flaws; yet I know those flaws coexist with the uniqueness of American opportunity. To disregard the value of American Universalism is to forgo the opportunity to learn from the past and pave a better path for others.

★

HUGH

My understanding of American Universalism comes from what I have learned from the late civil rights leader and Congressman John Lewis, with whom I was lucky to spend a meaningful amount of time while I was growing up.

When Congressman Lewis spoke of America's long, unfinished quest for justice and freedom, he combined deep love and hope with pragmatic realism. Quoting his friend Dr. King one moment and Hegel the next, Congressman Lewis framed history as "spiritual warfare between what is good and what is evil... between the forces of light and the forces of darkness."[1]

He knew that darkness better than most of us ever will. Beaten by police and mobs, jailed for nonviolent protest, he was no stranger to the terrible atrocities Americans can inflict upon each other. He remained a lifelong champion of getting into "good trouble" whenever injustice appeared.

Congressman Lewis also witnessed the triumph of light. He saw firsthand the journey from Selma's Bloody Sunday to the election of the first Black president. He forgave a man who apologized for having

---

1   Dear, J. (March 2021) "My long-lost conversation with John Lewis on his vision of nonviolence," *Waging Nonviolence*. https://wagingnonviolence.org/2021/03/long-lost-john-lewis-conversation-vision-for-culture-of-nonviolence/

once beaten him at a South Carolina bus station, and he urged everyone—regardless of race, creed, or ideology—to "love everyone."

Above all, he never stopped believing we could build Dr. King's "Beloved Community," in which all could thrive here in the United States. Acknowledging our nation's capacity for harm and moral failure did not, for him, invalidate the prospect of the American experiment or render that Beloved Community a utopian fantasy. He refused to excuse injustice, but likewise refused to excuse a surrender of hope for an America that works for all of its citizens.

American Universalism asks us to hold two important truths at once: that the United States has never fully lived up to its founding creed, and that its creed remains worth fighting for precisely because it contains the seeds of redemption. Hannah's family story, marked by sacrifice amid incarceration, reminds us how fear of each other can distort our ideals. Hugh's memories of John Lewis show how courage can realign us with them. Together they illuminate a paradox at the heart of our history: triumph and transgression—the light and the dark—travel side by side, and both are unmistakably ours.

Our generation, raised in an Internet age that foments outrage, nihilism, and tribalism, must reject both the nostalgia that airbrushes injustice and the fatalism that dismisses the prospect of an America that is both great and good. As heirs to the unfinished work and unmatched promise of the American experiment, we can choose to be stewards of renewal rather than curators of viral grievance: breaking free of outrage algorithms, seeing the full humanity in every neighbor, and recommitting each day to the practice of American Universalism—the conviction that each of us belongs within the circle of "We the People." By building coalitions wider than our wounds and stronger than our fears, we move closer to the Beloved Community that history and hope still insist is within reach. ★

★

Universalism From the Ground Up

True universalism starts at the local level, with stronger communities and families, civic pride, and a new focus on education.

The Future Is Engaged Pluralism

At the perilous intersection of politics, race, religion, and ethics, Americans need guidance. Institutions of higher learning can help forge our many identities and viewpoints into a shared—and pluralistic—future.

BY JONATHON S. KAHN

Professor of Religion, Africana, and American Studies, Vassar College

I've been teaching at Vassar College for more than 20 years. Here's my official title: Professor of Religion, Africana and American Studies. If I'm prodded to say a bit more about what I teach and write about, I will add: my work sits at the intersection of race, religious ethics, and American politics. Once when I introduced myself this way, someone wise said back to me: Be careful, because the thing about intersections is that they are where you're most likely to be hit. It was good advice because it is always advisable to be careful. But the question it raises is whether being careful should demand a retreat, a stepping back from the intersection altogether.

This is the question facing American higher education now, and my answer is a resounding no. Especially now, our institutions of higher learning have a responsibility to help us navigate the dangerous intersections we face, where fears about income inequality or job opportunities or migration or the environment lurk. Far from retreating, colleges and universities should be advancing, reviving the role that learning, inquiry and the cooperation must play if we are to build a shared future.

For a long time, the intersections built by the American educational community were seen as its strengths: as engines of scientific and technological growth; as allowing historical, literary, economic, and philosophical (to name just a few) imaginations to roam; and as opening up opportunities for anyone with desire and drive to join in learning. This, at least, is the story that higher ed has told itself, but it is becoming increasingly clear that the American public believes that higher education has in recent decades failed to live up to these strengths. This should alarm anyone who loves learning and who has seen the way education can change student's lives. Higher ed has to take responsibility for this erosion of trust.

But the current assault on American higher education is not trying to hold our institutions accountable to their missions. The withdrawing of funds for research and the monitoring of faculty and students for "viewpoint diversity"—to name just a few—are attacks on the idea that colleges and universities should be constructing complex intersections where people with different ideas, perspectives, and goals learn to work together. The question we face now is whether constructing these intersections is not only a valuable social good, but fundamental to what higher education understands as its core mission. The existential question we need to ask ourselves is how committed we are to continuing to build and nurture them.

For almost four years, I was the director of what Vassar calls its "Program in Engaged Pluralism." Instead of DEI, Vassar used the language of "engaged pluralism" to express the claim that intersections within an educational community need to be built around values of mutual respect. Engaged pluralism is based on two key and rather simple insights. First, a campus community holds multitudes. To quote Danielle Allen, "we are diverse in our identities and divergent in our ideologies." We are plural. Mutual respect demands that our community cannot be healthy unless our community's variedness feels welcomed, and each of us is responsible for our community's health. Second, feeling welcomed is not enough.

Mutual respect demands that we must build relationships and relationships only get built by doing things together, solving problems, and interacting with each other in practical and concrete ways. This is the *engaged* part of the engaged pluralism. All of us are responsible for engaging.

The engaged pluralism team surveyed the campus—not only students and faculty, but staff and administrators—and constructed working groups devoted to the common issues that the community was interested in. Issues included pedagogy and the curriculum, building bridges between campus and community, creating community through arts, and researching controversial issues in the college's past. Each working group always had a mix of students, faculty, and administrators on it, and they were free to invent and create projects by their own lights.

The working groups morphed over time, as new ideas were introduced and new questions emerged. Each stage was, by turns, thrilling (as projects took shape), frustrating (when projects invariably ran into challenges), and uniformly rewarding and transformative (as groups worked together to build projects that reflected their hopes and values). I think of our work in engaged pluralism as creating what scholars often call "civil society": diverse collections of citizens working voluntarily and according to values they find compelling for the sake of building stronger social bonds across the larger community.

The work these groups did together was remarkable. A storytelling project was formed, which fanned out across the campus to invite people to listen and talk to each other. The arts and community group resurrected a derelict billboard on the edge of campus and turned it into a rotating art gallery that featured Poughkeepsie artists on a monthly basis. The entire ninth grade of Poughkeepsie High School was invited onto campus for a "college day," where Vassar students ran workshops on what college was all about. Multiple projects dedicated to researching the college's archives led to several public events in which we all came together to think through how past practices—which in Vassar's case included racial discrimination and gender empowerment—could help us envision the work we want to do now.

There is nothing exclusively American about this project of engaged pluralism. Many societies have built and aspired to build mutual respect across a plurality of differences. But my involvement in engaged pluralism has had a particularly American lilt to it.

Over the last 20 years, what I have seen within certain academic circles is a deep reluctance to talk about the value American higher education brings to the American political project. The idea that higher education should contribute to our civic life has been thought to be not radical enough, too institution-oriented, seemingly aimed at producing compliant citizens instead of creative, thoughtful, and liberated social actors. This has always been a false binary, and the practices of engaged pluralism turn this on its head. Developing creative, thoughtful, and liberated social actors becomes radical inasmuch as it builds bonds—indeed, even institutional bonds—of mutual dependence. To build communities that value working with each other as a way to solve problems is vital work, work that reveals that we are not going to be able to survive without one another.

What is at stake in the project of engaged pluralism is not an abstract question of political theory, but, rather, the importance of the American system of higher education to the American body politic. The scholar Benedict Anderson teaches that all of us live and work within the gravitational pull of "imagined communities"—the people with whom we share cultural practices and political institutions. The imagined community of higher education and broader American society has long been one that touted its mutual obligations and contributions to each other. This imagined community valued education's role in achieving any number of different forms of societal excellence.

Right now, this imagined community is severely frayed, but I am unwilling to give up on its aspirations. Right now American higher education must devote itself to deeply considering whether it is living up to the role that it aspires to play—needs to play—in our society. And it needs to seek ways to renew this compact.

What if higher education did not teach merely the excellences of lab work, historical research, computer science, and all the other fields of knowledge? Higher education could also place at its core a project of engaged pluralism. Our institutions could teach radical versions of what Allen calls "political friendship... a set of hard-worn complicated habits that are used to bridge trouble, difficulty, and differences of personality, experience, and aspiration."

These sorts of habits and practices, which I think of as the habits and practices of relationship-building, have become atrophied in our American lives; maybe they were never robust in the first place. But what's surely the case—what we all know well—is that the intersections at which our differences exist are dangerous if we do not know how to navigate them. And if higher education is to renew its commitment to the American body politic, it has to teach us how to do this. It has to model and offer multiple ways to turn the legitimate fears and disagreements that exist at any intersection into actual experiences and projects that make visible our shared hopes for our collective good. ★

Real Freedom Starts with Community

To fulfill the promise of our rights as Americans,
they must be lived out in our neighborhoods,
communities, and shared digital spaces.

BY DEEPTI DOSHI

Co-director of New_ Public, a non-profit R&D lab
focused on creating healthy, prosocial digital spaces

When I was a kid, my parents told me stories about why they'd left India. They left during The Emergency, the period in the mid-1970s when Prime Minister Indira Gandhi suspended civil liberties, imprisoned student protestors and opposition leaders, censored the press, and ruled by decree. My parents weren't revolutionaries; they were hopeful immigrants, driven not just by fear of authoritarianism but by their belief in something better for themselves and their family. They came to the United States because they believed in the radical promise of freedom—freedom not just as an abstract concept, but as a way of life.

The words of the Declaration of Independence were a promise: of inalienable rights to liberty and the pursuit of happiness. To my parents these were not just lofty ideas, but a North Star. And while I now see the contradictions those words have always contained, I still believe, as my parents did, that their promise is worth fighting for.

But freedom doesn't become real just because it's written into founding documents. It has to be experienced—in neighborhoods, schools, libraries, and local digital spaces. It's in the daily work of building trust, solving problems together, and showing up for one another that we bring life to our universal ideals. That's the work of local community. And in this moment of national division and democratic uncertainty, it may be the most important work we have.

★

A NEW EMERGENCY IS HERE

We're in a different kind of emergency now in America. Democracy is teetering under the weight of cynicism, disinformation, and division. People feel increasingly disconnected from institutions that were meant to serve them. Meanwhile, the language of change can feel inaccessible and trapped in insider conversations that don't always speak to everyday concerns. Too often, we end up with movements that are either driven by fear or too abstract to reach the people who need them most.

In the face of these forces, we need a path that reconnects the universal ideals in the Declaration to everyday life. A path rooted in shared responsibility, common purpose, and our daily lives. One that affirms that everyone deserves freedom, rights, and opportunity, and that a pluralistic society is not only possible, but necessary. That we don't have to be the same for us to be in this together.

This is where our local communities can make the difference. Universalism gives us the "what": freedom, rights, and opportunity for all. But it's in our neighborhoods, towns, and gathering spaces—both physical and digital—that we are meant to experience the "how." When communities are strong, they translate big ideals into daily life through schools and libraries, small businesses and community boards, shared kitchens and neighborhood forums. But when communities are weak, those ideals stay out of reach. A thriving democracy depends on investing in the places where universal principles can become lived experiences.

Freedom is often framed as "freedom from." Freedom from tyranny, from interference, from control. But as economist and philosopher Amartya Sen has argued, freedom is also "freedom to." Freedom to live the kind of life you value, to participate, to build, and to shape the future alongside others. That is the kind of freedom my parents were looking for. And that kind of freedom only comes through community—through trust, built over time, and with the confidence that we can solve problems together while holding space for our differences.

COMMUNITY-ROOTED DEMOCRACY MAKES IDEALS REAL

Community-centered action brings freedom, rights, and opportunity to life in three fundamental ways. When we build strong local communities, we make big ideals real through daily results, shared effort, and the belief that we can shape what happens next.

Local Action Delivers Real Results in Everyday Life

Strong communities put decision-making power where people live. They invite us to create the rules, not just follow them. The freedoms in our founding documents can be a bit abstract. But when power is close at hand, freedom becomes participatory. It becomes real. Rights don't just live in courtrooms or on campaign posters. They live—or fail to live—in our schools, our shared outdoor spaces, our libraries, our streets.

Strong local communities create the conditions for rights to be experienced, not just written into law. In 2024, the Trust for Civic Life supported more than 100 rural programs across the U.S., helping local communities train leaders, create gathering spaces, and launch civic initiatives. In many cases, these efforts led to measurable gains in local engagement, with community members stepping into leadership roles for the first time.

Local structures like tenant unions, mutual aid groups, and neighborhood councils are often the first responders when broader systems fail. They're also the ones most accountable to the people they serve. To defend rights, we have to root them. That means building institutions that can withstand pressure and extend dignity, block by block—including in the digital spaces where so much of twenty-first-century life now unfolds. Just as we invest in local infrastructure offline, we need to do the same online: designing public spaces that are community-led, resilient, and built for care.

Being Together Builds Trust and Connection

Some might argue that local action alone can't address global challenges like climate change or economic inequality. They're right—but they miss how community-based work builds the relationships and habits that make broader collaboration possible. When communities practice democratic decision-making together, they develop the capacity and trust needed for coordination at every level.

We live in an age of alienation. Only 25 percent of Americans today believe that others can be trusted. Institutions are viewed with suspicion. Politics feels performative. Social media fuels outrage without offering real outlets for action. But when people work together to solve problems in the places they live, something shifts. Trust starts to grow again. The collective begins to feel possible.

Working side by side gives people a reason to show up, because they feel seen. That's how we start to reconnect democracy to identity and belonging.

Local Experience Builds Belief and Agency

Community-rooted action doesn't just make things better—it helps people see that change is possible. When you can see the impact of your voice, your vote, or your effort, democracy starts to feel like something real. This is how agency takes root.

When people help shape their communities—and see the fruits of that participation—they begin to believe in democracy again. They begin to believe in one another. From town-wide initiatives in Libby, Montana, to neighborhood efforts in the Imperial Valley, the Trust found that even small wins like public events or beautification projects can restore people's sense that things don't happen *to* them but *because* of them.

LOCAL DIGITAL SPACES CAN (AND MUST) SUPPORT THIS WORK

The same spirit that powers a neighborhood garden or community center can thrive online, if we design for it. As Robert Putnam documented 25 years ago in *Bowling Alone*, many of the social institutions that once formed the bedrock of American civic life, such as PTAs, faith groups, and neighborhood associations, have eroded over time. In their absence, people have turned to digital spaces for connection and shared purpose—especially local digital spaces where neighbors gather online to share news, organize efforts, and solve problems close to home.

At New_ Public, where I am a co-director, we're reimagining local digital spaces as essential civic infrastructure. These are the places where people now gather online to organize mutual aid, swap advice, share hyperlocal news, and hash out their neighborhood's future. But today, most of these digital gathering places are shaped by commercial platforms whose algorithms reward outrage over dialogue.

That's why we work closely with the community stewards who manage these spaces. These volunteer moderators and organizers do the invisible work of holding communities together. But the platforms they operate within often make that work harder, not easier. Their success depends not just on goodwill, but on support: training, tools, and thoughtful design that aligns with civic goals, not just ad revenue.

We've seen what's possible when these stewards are empowered. Through projects like our Neighborhood Steward Fellowship, we've brought together leaders of local online spaces from across the country to share practices, build networks, and imagine new models. The results are inspiring. But if we want this kind of locally focused digital infrastructure to thrive, we need structural change—including new incentives, new tools, and ownership models that prioritize the public good.

FREEDOM IS SOMETHING WE PRACTICE TOGETHER

American Universalism has always been a radical idea: that freedom belongs to everyone, that rights are universal, that opportunity is a guarantee. But these ideals aren't self-executing. They have to be built, block by block, thread by thread.

We can't meet this moment with fear or fatalism. We have to meet it with commitment. With presence. With courage. And with our neighbors.

As one of my favorite Buddhist teachers, Thich Nhat Hanh, reminds us, "We are here to awaken from our illusion of separateness." Freedom isn't something we fight for alone. It's something we practice together: in town halls and neighborhood meetings, in mutual aid networks and cooperatives, and in digital spaces designed for connection rather than extraction. The future of democracy depends not just on whom we elect, but on how deeply we are engaged with and can participate in the places we call home. ★

Touching Our Children's Hearts With Fire

When a nation is as fractured as ours is today,
the solution may be closer than we realize. We can rebuild
patriotism from the ground up—through family and
community—by harnessing the principles of universalism.

BY JASON MANGONE

Executive director, More in Common US

Other than the handful of passages that get repeated annually in the Catholic liturgy, there's only one text I re-read every year on the same day. Every Memorial Day, I spend 10 minutes with Oliver Wendell Holmes' 1884 Memorial Day Speech to a group of veterans in Keene, New Hampshire—a text that itself always thrusts me into prayer.

When I learned that Catalyst for American Futures' logo is the American flag of 1861, I knew that Holmes' speech would serve as the centerpiece of my contribution. That's because while Holmes eventually became a Supreme Court Justice, in July 1861 he received his commission into the 20th Massachusetts Regiment as a Second Lieutenant in the U.S. Army, beginning four years of service that saw him wounded three times in the Civil War.

A couple of decades after his war service, three years after he became famous by publishing the book *Common Law,* a year into his tenure on the Massachusetts Supreme Court, and 18 years before his appointment to the U.S. Supreme Court, Holmes opened his speech by explaining his prompt: "Not long ago I heard a young man ask why people still kept up Memorial Day, and it set me thinking of the answer. Not the answer that you and I should give to each other—not the expression of those feelings that, so long as you and I live, will make this day sacred to memories of love and grief and heroic youth—but an answer which should command the assent of those who do not share our memories, and in which we of the North and our brethren of the South could join in perfect accord."

His response to the question "Why should we keep Memorial Day?" is that the memory of youthful passion ought to serve as an inspiration to those who were fortunate enough not to have been required to serve in an awful war. Holmes' language is much more stirring. In a passage worth quoting at length, he implores:

> "When we meet thus, when we do honor to the dead in terms that must sometimes embrace the living, we do not deceive ourselves. We attribute no special merit to a man for having served when all were serving. We know that if the armies of our war did anything worth remembering, the credit belongs not mainly to the individuals who did it, but to average human nature. We also know very well that we cannot live in associations with the past alone, and we admit that if we would be worthy of the past we must find new fields for action or thought and make for ourselves new careers.

> "But, nevertheless, the generation that carried on the war has been set apart by its experience. Through our great good fortune, in our youth our hearts were touched with fire. It was given to us to learn at the outset that life is a profound and passionate thing....

"We have seen with our own eyes beyond and above the gold fields the snowy heights of honor, and it is for us to bear the report to those who come after us. But above all, we have learned that whether a man accepts from Fortune her spade, and will look downward and dig, or from Aspiration her axe and cord, and will scale the ice, the one and only success which it is his to command is to bring to his work a mighty heart."

I was lucky enough to have had the opportunity to serve my country. I was a senior in high school on September 11, 2001, and by the time I graduated college and took my commission into the Marine Corps, the country was at war in Iraq and Afghanistan. For me and all of my dearest friends, military service was an easy and obvious choice in the early 2000s. As Holmes explains, I was fortunate to "learn at the outset that life is a profound and passionate thing." I rarely meet that high bar for sincerity, but it is the bar I've learned to set for myself.

As a father of four, my annual re-read of Holmes' speech now leads to prayerful contemplation on the question: "What might touch my children's hearts with fire?" Out of tragedy, the world gave me a worthy field of endeavor early in life. It's been a quarter-century since September 11, a decade or more since the wars in Iraq and Afghanistan became obviously misguided ventures, and five years since a pandemic became the first national emergency that failed to bring us more tightly together as a nation. It's not clear to me that we're still capable of producing patriotic conviction at scale. And yet, like my family did for me, I can try to guide my own children to such conviction.

With Holmes' speech as my inspiration, these are the few ways I'm trying to mold my own children's patriotism. What follows is not a political program, but a very personal one. And while it centers around my children, the general point is to focus deeply wherever you have the most intimate relationships, whether you have children or not.

The basic rhythms of my family's life made it impossible to mistake the modern world's markers of success as anything more than fleeting.

Every Sunday my family went to Mass together and then convened for an early-afternoon meal. Although I couldn't articulate it as such until my late twenties, rituals like these made it impossible to believe that anything in life was more profound than the community around our table, or that any measure of success mattered more than having earned my family's respect. As I've grown older, I've realized that sitting around that table, eating the same meal, and blessing the meal with the same prayer, oriented my life to something deeper, more ancient, more eternal than mere achievement. I have more years of post-secondary education than my grandmother had of any schooling whatsoever. But as the oldest cousin of my generation, I can easily say that the smartest thing I've ever done was spending a few afternoons with my grandmother before her dementia took her faculties from her, learning how she made the Sunday meal. I remember very few of the things anyone in my family ever told me, but being at the same table every week shapes my moral code. Continuing that tradition for my own family, especially so in a world in which such tradition seems anachronistic, is vital. I suppose the idea is to take practical steps (literally, making sauce and meatballs and eating that every Sunday after going to Mass) to connect my children to something eternal.

I can teach my kids that they ought to love their country. The two sides of my family are very different—one side has been here for hundreds of years, with roots in the South and in West Virginia; the other side arrived from Italy in 1955. For one side America is the family's roots; on the other America was an idea, then an opportunity, then a home. These are very different streams that feed into the same river of gratitude. I want my kids to know it's righteous to love their country.

I can show my kids what it looks like to be committed to their community, and that politics and power aren't central to a good life. Shortly before my first son was born, an organization I was working for received an award at the Clinton Global Initiative and I got to shake the former president's hand on the stage. Since I've had kids, I've had the opportunity to meet with many other *very important people*. My kids don't care. On the other hand, I'm a local volunteer firefighter and very involved with my local Little League, where I coach a few teams and sit on the board. My kids have never mentioned my work, but they consistently talk about the stuff they see me doing around town.

Holmes' speech moves me to tears because it gives life to the idea that patriotic action helped him—and his generation—understand that life is a sacred thing, an opportunity not to be missed. It is an ideal of citizenship. Early in the speech, he says: "We know that if the armies of our war did anything worth remembering, the credit belongs not mainly to the individuals who did it, but to average human nature." The war gave innate patriotism a place to express itself—we might often express our patriotism in the wake of tragedy or in the midst of war, but Holmes' point was that the patriotism itself was already there. I'm not certain that average human nature in 2025 is capable of the self-sacrifice that Holmes described as commonplace 150 years ago.

There has always been a sort of simplicity in the ideal of American life. If the points I've tried to make sound old-fashioned—that habits matter, that it's good to love your country, and that getting involved in your local community is the most important thing you can do—then it sort of makes my point. These habits used to be baked into our very way of being. In the modern world, we have to work to cultivate them and pass them on. ★

★

Imagining a New American Future

Yielding to tyranny is not an option.
There are paths forward—diverse, uncertain,
even messy—but we must find common ground.
Universalism can show us the way.

I Brought the Flag Home

In the days before the Civil War, a new flag became a symbol of the struggle for freedom. Today that symbol still applies—perhaps more than ever—to agree on, and articulate, the shared principles that allow us to say what we are for.

BY ERIC K. WARD

Executive vice president of Race Forward,
senior fellow at the Southern Poverty Law Center,
and the only American recipient of the Civil Courage Prize

From 2017 to 2021, the streets of Portland felt like the frontline of something bigger than simple street protests. Paramilitary violence and harassment unfolded with increasing intensity. Armed and unarmed groups descended in the name of Trumpism. Not as supporters of free speech, but as intimidators, agitators, and enforcers of a political vision that included threatening Portland residents with training-grade impact arms and wearing images of people who disagreed with them being thrown from helicopters.

When Trump's federal agents arrived, uninvited, violence escalated. For a moment, it felt like Portland had been abandoned by the rest of the country, left to stand alone against a creeping storm.

But here's what surprises people: In that moment, I didn't find my patriotism—I just expressed it more confidently. I reaffirmed something I've believed all my life, even when this country tried to teach me otherwise. As Pauli Murray once wrote, *"Hope is a song in a weary throat."* My throat was weary—but the song had never stopped.

I'm part of a long tradition of Black American patriots—people who believed in the promise of this nation and demanded that it live up to that promise. People who knew that love of country didn't mean silence in the face of injustice. It meant organizing, struggling, showing up—for the vote, for our communities, for each other.

In that spirit I went looking for a symbol not of nostalgia, but of insistence. I found the 1861 American flag. Thirty-four stars. A flag that flew in the very year this nation fractured under the weight of white supremacy, insurrection, and defense of chattel slavery, but also the year we chose to fight for a broader democracy. The year we refused to let the idea of *"government of the people"* be hijacked by aristocrats. I brought that flag home—not as a discovery, but as a declaration: We've been here before, and we know what must be done.

That flag symbolized what I will now say plainly: I believe in American Universalism not because I've been blind to this nation's failures, but because I've lived through them and still choose to believe in the people who keep trying. I'm a Black man, a product of the Los Angeles public schools, a survivor of both segregation and desegregation. I've seen what exclusion looks like and I've experienced what mutual accountability feels like. Universalism, to me, isn't about erasing identity. It's about building a power that doesn't require someone else to lose theirs. It doesn't mean pretending we're all the same. It means building a tangible democratic republic strong enough to hold all of who we are.

Like Southern aristocrats, adherents of Trumpism have co-opted the language of revolution. They talk of patriotism while waving flags soaked in authoritarianism, violence, and exclusion. They speak of freedom while seeking to control what we learn, how we vote, who we associate with, and what we believe. They build movements not around hope, but around fear—fear of self-determination, of change, of one another.

And yet, too often, the movements that claim the moral high ground—left, liberal, or principled conservative opposition—have struggled to articulate what we stand for beyond the idea that we oppose Trumpism. We've been quick to critique, slow to cohere. Loud about our differences, quiet about what unites us. We've mistaken ideological purity for clarity, and ideological alienation for strategy. And in that vacuum, Americans—particularly young men—have turned elsewhere, seduced by false strength and manufactured grievance.

It's not enough to be against Trumpism or other forms of authoritarianism. Not anymore. What we need now—what we've always needed—is a set of shared commitments we're willing to build with people we don't always agree with, but who are ready to stand shoulder to shoulder anyway.

So let me be clear about what I stand for:

Universal Freedom. Freedom from coercion. Freedom from racial terror and economic exploitation. Freedom to live, speak, worship, and love—without fear. That includes the freedom to dissent and to imagine a life different from your neighbor's without threatening theirs.

Universal Rights. I believe in rights that apply to every person regardless of race, gender, religion, or origin—because rights that only apply to some are not rights at all. Black Americans, immigrants, Jews, Muslims, LGBTQ+ people, rural workers—we have all been scapegoated by systems and narratives that thrive on division. Universal rights are the antidote to authoritarian logic.

Universal Opportunity. We deserve an economy that doesn't grind people down or pretend that dignity is a luxury. That includes housing, healthcare, education, and food—not as charity, but as the foundation of a functioning democracy. A society that treats these as optional is not built for all of us. It is built to exclude.

This isn't just policy. It's personal. My life has been shaped by people who believed that democracy only works when it works for everyone. By mentors who saw organizing not as careerism but as care work. By scenes—from punk to policy rooms—where people believed change was possible if we stuck with each other long enough to make it real.

That's the kind of patriotism I believe in. Not blind allegiance or pseudo-exceptionalism. I mean fierce love. Love strong enough to call out injustice. Love brave enough to confront the authoritarian impulse in ourselves and our institutions. Love clear-eyed about our history and still willing to build something better.

That 1861 flag I brought home to Portland was born in a fractured moment not unlike our own. Then, as now, the country faced a choice: democracy for some or democracy for all. The Civil War did not fully deliver on the latter, but it cracked the illusion that we could ever go backward and call it freedom. And today, as Trumpism corrodes the republic from within, we are again being asked to choose.

So, what comes next?

We need new movements and leaders rooted in majority politics, not purity politics. Movements and leaders that meet people where they are without leaving them where they are. Movements and leaders that organize not only through identity, but through shared values—values like fairness, dignity, courage, and curiosity.

E pluribus unum—from many, one—was never a truth fulfilled in this country. It was a slogan engraved in stone while slavery stood, a motto spoken over centuries of exclusion. But it wasn't meaningless. It was a provocation. A challenge. And for some of us—for Black Americans, for immigrants, for anyone pushed to the edges—it was a banner we refuse to surrender.

Not because America had lived up to it, but because we weren't ready to give up on what it could mean. And we weren't alone. Some in the majority—abolitionists, freedom riders, union builders, whistleblowers, quiet neighbors—chose to build a country that would finally mean what it said. That's the work of American Universalism—not pretending we've arrived, but refusing to abandon the only road worth walking together.

That's what American Universalism offers us: a North Star that does not erase difference but unites us in a common purpose. That path ahead will not be won by shouting louder or retreating into silos. It will be won by reclaiming patriotism, rebuilding trust, and defending democracy on every front—from school boards to social media, from kitchen tables to capitol steps.

And as Ella Baker reminded us, *"Strong people don't need strong leaders."* We just need a chance to act together.

So, what fights would I pick?

First, reclaim public education—not as a culture war battlefield, but as democracy's training ground. Trumpism seeks to transform public education into a control mechanism—where fear replaces discipline, censorship flattens complexity, and diversity is scrubbed from the American story. We need to defend educators, protect honest history, and build a movement of students, parents, and teachers who believe that truth-telling is patriotism. If we lose the ability to teach our past, we'll never build the future.

Second, defend local government. Authoritarians always start by discrediting the local—the school board, the city council, the library board. Why? Because that's where people first practice democracy. That's where trust is either built or broken. Let's flip the script. Let's make local governance a site of belonging, competence, and bold civic action. We can't just rely on Washington—we win when we lead from where we live.

Third, disrupt the isolation economy. The far right thrives in loneliness. In grievance. In the feeling that no one sees you or cares what happens next. We need to fight back with joy. With music. With meals. With mutual aid. With gatherings that aren't just about protest but about presence. In a time of political despair, community is a counteroffensive.

We've seen it before—in jazz clubs and basement shows, in barber shops and book clubs, in mosques and union halls. Places where we made something out of nothing, and something became home.

These aren't just issues. They're leverage points. Each one is a place where we can change the rules, grow majorities, and remind people that freedom isn't something we inherit—it's something we practice.

We've seen this kind of courage up close. On January 6, 2021, Capitol Police officer Eugene Goodman didn't give a speech. He didn't carry a sign. But his actions—diverting Trump insurrectionists away from the Senate chamber with nothing but a calm, steady voice—reminds us that standing your ground for democracy doesn't always look like a movement. Sometimes, it's just one person in the hallway saying: Not here.

The story we need isn't about left or right. It's about whether we still believe in each other enough to build something better—knowing full well we've all messed up along the way and still choosing to begin again.

So yes, I'm flying that 1861 flag—not to mourn the nation we've lost, but to fight for the one we're still becoming.

I didn't bring that flag home because I was nostalgic. I brought it home because I needed something to carry with me. Something to hold onto while we face a movement that's trying—once again—to strip this country down to fear, silence, and disappearance. And what we do next will decide what survives.

Because I know what happens if we don't.

That's my patriotism.

That's my universalism.

That's my answer. ★

The Research University as a Bastion of Democracy

Our universities have a role in sustaining democracy, but that role is under threat—not only by external attacks but by internal confusion. Civic values need to be returned to campus so that graduates are prepared to assume the mantle of democracy.

BY NILS GILMAN

COO & EVP at the Berggruen Institute and former associate chancellor, UC Berkeley

The American research university is on the ropes. Forget the ivy-covered nostalgia; these institutions are facing a political onslaught, spearheaded by MAGA forces who rightly perceive them as key pillars of cultural and political opposition. This isn't hyperbole. Look at the authoritarian playbook worldwide: from Bolsonaro to Orbán to Erdoğan, defunding and purging universities is standard procedure. Chris Rufo's gutting of New College in Florida wasn't an isolated incident; it was explicitly a beta test for a national campaign. The targeting starts with DEI and the eradication of critical inquiry into race, gender, equity, and social justice from the curriculum but will end with the eradication of academic freedom and scientific inquiry generally, enforced by the blunt instrument of federal funding threats.

This incoming assault, threatening the intellectual foundations of democratic society, is landing on a vulnerable target. Universities today find themselves politically isolated, sniped at from all sides. The right decries them as "woke indoctrination factories" pushing "communist" ideas. The left sees them as engines of neoliberalism, saddling graduates with debt while partnering with corporations. Libertarians dismiss them as antiquated credentialing mills divorced from real-world value. The post-Cold War, post-New Deal consensus that saw universities as vital national assets, worthy of bipartisan investment, has evaporated–and with it an opportunity to investigate and develop the concepts of universal truths and freedom.

Amidst this multi-front siege, the critical question for university leaders—and for anyone concerned about the health of democratic society—is how to preserve and enhance what is *uniquely valuable* about the research university. What core functions do these institutions perform better than any other, functions whose loss would grievously wound society?

Universities have three core competencies: the creation of highly trained experts, path-breaking knowledge creation, and the preservation and transmission of existing knowledge. Notice what's *not* on this list: the remediation of historic wrongs or the direct promotion of social justice. While these may be worthy goals, they are not tasks for which the research university possesses a unique institutional advantage. Those battles are better fought through explicit political processes or by civil society organizations with clear moral mandates. Conflating the university's core intellectual mission—the rigorous pursuit and preservation of systematic truth, or *Wissenschaft*—with a generalized social justice agenda dilutes its purpose and weakens its defenses.

It's within these core competencies that the university's profound, though often poorly articulated, importance to democracy resides. John Dewey observed a deep structural alignment between the practices of science and the principles of democracy. Both, he noted, fundamentally reject arguments from authority. Both rely on open inquiry, the free exchange of ideas, transparency of method, and—perhaps most crucially—built-in mechanisms for self-correction. Evidence and reasoned argument, not dogma or diktat, are the coin of the realm. Disagreements are to be hashed out civilly, and adjudicated on the basis of shared facts. Errors are not heresies to be suppressed, but opportunities for revision and improvement.

The research university, at its best, is the institutional embodiment of this Deweyan ideal. Knowledge creation within its walls—the process of research—is predicated on skepticism, peer review (a formalized system of critique), and the constant testing of hypotheses against evidence. This process is inherently anti-authoritarian. It thrives on dissent and challenges to established orthodoxies. When universities function correctly, they are practicing a form of democratic epistemology in microcosm, a stark contrast to the top-down, authority-based knowledge systems favored by illiberal regimes.

Furthermore, the university's role in training experts is not merely about producing skilled technocrats. It's about cultivating minds capable of critical analysis, evidence evaluation, and reasoned judgment—capacities essential for an informed citizenry capable of navigating the firehose of disinformation that characterizes contemporary politics. Expertise generated through open, rigorous, and self-correcting processes provides a vital bulwark against propaganda and politically motivated falsehoods.

Finally, the function of knowledge preservation and transmission, particularly within the humanities, is indispensable for democratic health. A renewed humanities should focus not on endlessly remediating the past's sins, but on preserving and transmitting what is worthy about the past. This is not a call for uncritical veneration. Rather, it's a recognition that democratic societies require deep historical consciousness, cultural memory, and access to diverse intellectual traditions to understand the present, imagine different futures, and resist the simplistic, often barbaric narratives peddled by authoritarians. A citizenry cut off from what Matthew Arnold called the "greatest and best" of past thought—across all cultures—is easily manipulated.

Academics, by virtue of their specialized knowledge and roles within institutions of higher learning, often occupy a position as intellectual elites. However, their crucial practice of rigorously seeking and conveying truths should not serve to merely entrench the privileges and elitism of the academy. Instead, this pursuit of understanding and its dissemination should actively support and empower democratic participation by making complex information accessible, fostering critical thinking among the broader public, and contributing to informed civic discourse. When academics prioritize public engagement, clear communication, and research that addresses societal challenges, they fulfill a vital democratic function, ensuring that knowledge serves as a foundation for collective decision-making rather than remaining confined within an ivory tower.

However, the university's capacity to perform these democracy-sustaining functions is currently compromised, not only by external attacks but by internal weaknesses. Various critiques of the academy—the crushing cost burden, the potential irrelevance of certain modes of teaching and research, the embrace of "activist scholarship" at the expense of *Wissenschaft*, and the crisis of purpose within the humanities—are not merely trivial quibbles. They represent significant failures of the institution to adapt to contemporary realities and, crucially, to articulate and defend its core value proposition in the current political landscape.

The escalating cost of higher education fuels populist resentment and lends credence to claims that universities are merely elite playgrounds detached from societal needs. The blurring of lines between scholarship and activism provides ammunition to those who claim universities are biased indoctrination centers, eroding public trust in academic expertise. And the failure of the humanities, in many quarters, to embrace their vital role in preserving and transmitting cultural knowledge, opting instead for a primary focus on critique and remediation, leaves them vulnerable to defunding and perceived irrelevance. These internal failings provide openings for anti-intellectual and authoritarian actors who are seeking not to reform but to dismantle the university system wholesale.

Saving the research university, therefore, requires more than fending off the immediate political onslaught. It demands a clear-eyed internal reckoning. Universities must address their operational and financial models. They need to rigorously defend principles of free inquiry while maintaining high standards for scholarly rigor, pushing back against trends that subordinate the pursuit of truth to political or social agendas. And the humanities must reclaim their essential role as curators and transmitters of civilizational knowledge, understanding this not as a retreat from relevance, but as a core contribution to critical thought and democratic resilience.

Ultimately, defending the research university is not about protecting institutional inertia or academic privilege. It is about safeguarding a vital space where the Deweyan principles of democratic inquiry—the rejection of authority, the commitment to evidence, the embrace of critique, and the capacity for self-correction—can be practiced and propagated. These principles are the antithesis of the authoritarianism gaining ground globally. A ruthless focus on the core competencies that embody these principles—expert training, knowledge creation, and knowledge preservation—is the university's best, perhaps only, defense against the barbarians both outside and inside the gates. The stakes are far higher than departmental budgets or academic prestige; they concern the intellectual foundations of democratic society itself. ★

Storytellers on Democracy's Front Lines

The stories we choose to tell about ourselves play a critical role in defining who we are. As we search for connection, empathy, and humanity in this deeply divided time, look to storytellers to help us embrace pluralism.

BY STEVEN OLIKARA

President, Bridge Entertainment Labs

★

At a time when the media industry—both entertainment and news—is going through a fundamental overhaul, we must reckon with a fundamental question that will shape the future of our democracy: Which stories do we choose to tell about ourselves, and which do we overlook?

We're living in times when the American story is often framed as a WWE-style match between Team Red and Team Blue, where a vortex of polarization sucks nearly every topic into each side's ideological script. Although addictive for many, and profitable for some, this cultural frame is disastrous for our democracy and our personal lives. That frame also ignores America's foundational idea of *E Pluribus Unum:* Out of many, one.

More than ever, we must transform "us vs. them" into a new story of us—a story that weaves together the frayed American social fabric. To those skeptical of bridging America's divides through transactional compromises, I am with you. This moment calls for a different approach, and we need to tap into a deeper way of connecting across differences. The idea of pluralism captures this spirit. When building bridges with a pluralistic mindset, the goal is not necessarily to meet at the 50-yard line. It's about meeting on a new playing field, the result of listening to one another's stories.

A new storytelling arc is now emerging to accomplish exactly that—one that embraces pluralism and cultivates a real desire to hear other people's lived experiences. And the storytelling industry—screenwriters, producers, directors—has a unique platform to foster this kind of connection.

At this year's Sundance Film Festival, for instance, the documentary series *Bucks County, USA* premiered. Directed by Oscar winner Barry Levinson and Robert May, this series follows the friendship of two 14-year-old girls from politically divergent families, illustrating that beneath our political labels there's a common human thread. Films like the Oscar-winning *A Real Pain* showcase characters who, through their struggles and triumphs, remind us of our shared humanity. These stories don't just entertain; they show us how to relate to each other, proving that narrative can be a powerful tool for social cohesion.

In today's global landscape, where confidence in traditional media has waned, entertainment storytelling emerges as a key to rebuilding trust in one another. It's not about pushing an agenda; it's about sharing narratives that are deeply rooted in American communities, authentically reflecting our cultural zeitgeist. At this moment, the most insightful storytellers are asking, "What am I missing?" and tapping into the curiosities of the American public from all walks of life.

America, like the best stories, is inherently complex. The journey to thriving together in a free and pluralistic society involves seeing the humanity in each other and building constructive engagement across our differences. This is hard work, but essential in the most diverse nation in human history. Our Founding Fathers knew this, navigating profound differences to create a lasting system of self-government. The storytelling industry can learn from America's founding idea of pluralism, using conflict to drive narratives toward creating a common understanding.

That's why storytellers are on the front lines of our democracy. The magic of storytelling creates a unique kind of transportation. We let our guard down while becoming immersed in the characters' journey. When those stories portray nuanced characters who don't fit into expected roles or viewpoints, they change how we see the world.

As someone who's walked the line between politics and culture, I see storytelling as an ongoing act of civic engagement. Voting takes place in a single moment, but engaging with your community, understanding your neighbors, and sharing your experiences are daily democratic acts. Your stories are a form of civic participation. They educate, they challenge, and they heal.

Remember: The American stories we choose to tell are the stories that shape us. To all storytellers, from our local communities to the biggest studios, let's choose to tell bold stories that explore the beauty, complexity, and challenge of finding our shared humanity. We are a nation that's desperate for connection. Let's retether the American fabric by making new "stories of us" a cultural phenomenon that cannot be ignored. ★

When Monsters Are Rampant, Summon Your Heroes

Reclaiming institutions from corruption and
authoritarianism is possible. It has happened before,
and it can happen now.

BY SALLY VANCE-TREMBATH

Teaching professor in Catholic Theology at Santa Clara University

Human rights are not a recent invention. As far back as the proph-
ets of the Hebrew Bible and Christ's description of the Reign of God,
there have been proclamations of the dignity and value of each and every
human person. Communities of faith have powered some of the most
successful human rights movements in the United States, yet many people today who claim social justice as their work are unfamiliar with that
history. One of my frustrations as a theologian has been how ignorance
of previous work undermines the current movement, and how we under-
value the heroes who have done that work for millennia.

The work of human rights has always required robust, stable institutions that are not simply a cluster of functions—they are powered by
heroes. These "garden variety" heroes do their work carefully, and they
do it for the sake of goodness.

When I think of heroes I always think of a nurse practitioner named Jean, who I met in my first year in San Francisco. She was a wise woman—a former nun who had changed her profession to respond to the AIDS plague. I had become quite ill, and Jean diagnosed my job as the source of my health problems. She was right. My workplace was a hostile environment, and it was literally making me sick.

"Get out of there," she said. "You cannot change that institution; you have to find one that values your work." At this point her gaze, which was already quite direct, shifted to a deeper level and she asked: "Who are your champions? While you find a new job, summon your heroes."

It took me a minute to understand that she meant champions from my own inner life.

By the end of the appointment, Jean had prescribed two kinds of medicine: one chemical and the other spiritual. The pharmacy could supply the first, but for the other I needed something else. My assaulted brain needed therapy, too, as did my bruised spirit. I was suffering from an institutional toxin. As I left that day, Jean told me, "Summon your heroes to protect you from the monsters."

During our time when so many institutions are either failing or are mistrusted, we need the stories of heroes like Jean to inspire us as we go about the work of rebuilding. Our heroes are the ones who help us face down the monsters.

And monsters do abound. Just look at the stories of the Jewish and Christian traditions, both of which tell us about monsters who undermine the value of others. The stories often rely on the personification of evil: Satan. In John Milton's luxurious description of the story, Lucifer—the most light-filled angel—rejected God's commitment to the human community. As Lucifer saw it, any creature who was limited by a body should not be given an intellect. This anti-human view got Lucifer kicked out of God's presence.

One cannot be a "messenger of God" if one denies God's essential goodness, so Lucifer became "the Lord of the Flies, the Prince of

Darkness." In other words, a monster. Jean knew from monsters, and knew they didn't live only in Bible stories.

So what should we do when monsters take over institutions? My counsel as one who studies the reform movements within Catholicism: When monsters run rampant, stay in your lane and look for the heroes.

I study the nature and mission of the Catholic Church; that is my lane. My particular focus is the Second Vatican Council's history and texts, and the consequences of that reforming council. My focus is the institutional Church, so I know well the importance of heroes—especially when institutions are called upon to change. We can use Vatican II as a model for facing down monsters and effecting change in even the largest institutions.

Staying in your own lane is not common in our modern society. Social media encourages people to occupy any and all lanes; actual competence is undermined. It is not a fancy to see social media platforms as monsters: Hydras of destruction, masquerading as a common space. Yes, monsters are masters of disguise.

In order for heroes to help, they need to be visible, recognizable. Vatican II was an historic institutional reform project that focused on humanity. With the Council as my academic center of gravity, a neuralgic issue for me is the poor understanding of what Vatican II *did* and what it actually *said*.

If asked about the signal reforms of the Council, many Catholics would cite the concept of the Church as "the People of God" or the move away from Latin as the language used in the Mass. While these are certainly features of the Council's reforms, reducing the Council to them minimizes the extent to which it was a paradigm shift. The scaffold of the Council's teaching is its return to the Hebrew Bible and the People of Israel's genius: People are made in the image and likeness of God. That *imago Dei* had been defeated by a false dualism between body and spirit that Augustine and others brought to Christianity from Greek philosophy. Over time, that dualism was reinforced at the expense of a recognition that our identity comes from our relationship with God, the source of all goodness.

In all creation we are distinctly connected to God by our capacity to make intentional moves for the sake of goodness. Our finite bodies and our infinite spirits both contribute to our capacity for growing in goodness. The dualism that shaped Augustine and his theological kin led to an overemphasis on the biological and physical at the expense of the spiritual. That plays out as "the body is bad; the spirit is good." That characterization of our humanity provided the scaffold for some untenable teachings.

Vatican II privileged the human capacities for relationships that run from the Creation story through Aquinas' insight about the cooperation between the human and the divine. When we creatures are seen as participating in the very activities that mark God's character—loving, learning, creating beauty, and striving for excellence—the body ceases to be the primary category. Our bodies become our friends. We pay more attention to them not because they are doorways to sin but because our dignity lies in our distinct configuration of finite creatures with infinite capacities.

In theological jargon this is known as theological anthropology. It was the theological anthropology of the Council that led to the new institution that is still emerging. We know from deeply tragic recent experience that elements of the pre-modern church still lurk in the shadows. Old paradigms die hard.

How can we apply the lessons of theological anthropology to our political institutions? Jean had told me to look out for monsters, but we need to ask, What makes a monster? What are its features?

The answer is that monsters may be misshapen in many different ways, but they all share one distinctive feature: they are destroyers. Sadly, institutions often provide cover for monsters.

Vatican II provides us with insight into our need for robust institutions. Long before the current assault on the government's commitment to human rights and the common good of its citizens, I had been pondering similar failures in the Catholic Church. It was indeed doing monstrous things. It was teaching that the denominations of the Reformation were not actual churches but "heretical communities;" that the "perfidious

Jews killed Christ;" and that the millions of human beings in the Muslim, Buddhist, and atheist communities would not be "saved." Those are not just incoherent teachings, they are monstrous—because they deny the very foundation that Catholicism claimed to serve: God's all-encompassing love for the entire human community throughout history, which is displayed in our inherent dignity.

Jean is one of my personal heroes, but we also need famous, public heroes. Mine is the institutional reformer Pope John XXIII, who called and guided the Second Vatican Council. That council marked the Catholic Church's tardy entrance into direct dialogue with modernity.

Pope John recognized that the institutional Church was serving itself, instead of the human community. He knew that institutions serve people, not the other way round. That's the direction in which we need to move our secular institutions as well.

Before Pope John's shrewd move toward reform, the Catholic Church had developed many exclusionary tendencies. Pope John knew that because the institution was still functioning through its medieval, pre-modern worldview, it was failing in its mission of serving the entire human community. The worldview had replaced the mission. This is the challenge of institutions: their structure provides stability but that stability can shift away from its mission. When that happens the structure's own existence replaces its outward-facing work.

What was Pope John's first move toward institutional reform? He articulated the Church's mission and proclaimed it clearly, with energy and enthusiasm and joy. His move became embedded in many of the Council's documents.

"The joys and hopes, the grief and anguish of the people of our time, especially those who are poor or afflicted, are the joys and hopes, the grief and anguish of the followers of Christ as well. Nothing that is genuinely human fails to find and echo in their hearts. For theirs is the community of people united in Christ and guided by the Holy Spirit in their pilgrimage towards the Father's kingdom, bearers of a message of salvation for all humanity. That is why they cherish a feeling of deep solidarity with the human race and its history."

— "The Pastoral Constitution on the Church in the Modern World," *Gaudium et spes*

Pope John's second move was to draw upon the wisdom of actual authorities instead of just functionaries. Apparatchiks are their own special brand of monsters. Before Pope John, the Vatican bureaucracy was filled with functionaries in offices that had little or no interest in the actual experiences of Catholics in the modern situation.

One of the experts that Pope John elevated was John Courtney Murray, the American Jesuit who had been writing about how the U.S. Constitution might provide a template for the Catholic Church's thinking on freedom of religious practice. Murray had been previously silenced; the very ideas that triggered his silencing became the official teaching of the Catholic Church in "Declaration on Religious Liberty," *Dignitatis humanae.*

"People nowadays are becoming increasingly conscious of the dignity of the human person; a growing number demand that people should exercise their own judgment and a responsible freedom in the actions and should not be subject to external pressure or coercion but inspired by a sense of duty. At the same time, to prevent excessive restrictions of the rightful freedom of individuals and associations, they demand constitutional limitation of the powers of government."

— *Dignitatis humane*

The universalist values that the Catalyst for American Futures hopes to proclaim and implement have deep roots in all faith traditions, but especially the Gospel of Jesus Christ, which is itself a distillation of the profound insight of the People of Israel. We are not members of separate tribes; we belong to the one human family. The Christian and Jewish communities have been calling out the monsters of power and tribalism long since. Their work is a rich resource for today's work. Monsters are eventually brought to justice and communities have to persevere in their commitment to keeping institutions on track and in service to us, not for us to be in service to them.

Let me close with one more story of an everyday hero. I have lived in San Francisco for more than 20 years, but I am a child of the Midwest. When I was 13, I made an ill-advised swim across the Mississippi from Iowa to Illinois, at a point where that river is indeed mighty. The swim was beyond my abilities. But my neighbor Steve, a member of a high school swim team that routinely sent its graduates to elite colleges, said he was going to swim across and he thought that I could as well. Even my reckless 13-year-old self knew that if I got into trouble Steve would help me. Knowing a hero was at hand, I made the swim.

Heroes like Steve provide the strength and support we need to discover that we are more capable than we might realize. That, too, is evidence of the claim that we are made in God's image. But his personal heroism was born of his being part of that champion swim team—the institution that supported Steve swam invisibly alongside us that day.

We need to revivify the connection between small moments like these and the institutions that undergird them. Institutions may create monsters, but they also create the heroes we can call on to defeat them. ★

The Mosque

Much more than a place of worship, this Ohio building
is a symbol of belonging, a marker of endurance that
anchors a community to its adopted home.

BY SHAMILA N. CHAUDHARY
Foreign policy professional

★

In the northwest corner of Ohio, where the highways braid together
and the horizon stretches without ambition, two minarets rise. They don't
dominate the skyline—they interrupt it, gently. Their silhouette might
belong to Istanbul, or Lahore, or Beirut. But they stand in Perrysburg,
surrounded by cornfields and strip malls, holding their ground with
quiet clarity.

The Islamic Center of Greater Toledo arrived in the early 1980s,
but its roots run deeper—into the loam of migration, memory, and long-
ing. To outsiders, the mosque may seem like an import. To those of us
who grew up here, it's a landmark of return.

My parents came to Toledo from Pakistan in 1980. I was two. My
mother says the sky in Ohio reminded her of Punjab—wide, unboth-
ered, endless. The fields were familiar, too, but the stillness felt different. In Pakistan, General Zia-ul-Haq had just begun to narrow the public
imagination, reshaping the country's identity under the weight of state
religion. In America, Jimmy Carter—a peanut farmer with a preacher's

cadence—was wrapping up his presidency. We had fled one kind of certainty for another: from the rigidity of ideology to the mess of democracy.

Crossing over meant leaving things behind—extended family, the grammar of communal life, a sense of place so deep it had no name. What we found instead were the bare tools of American living: mortgages, school buses, job applications, polite neighbors. No village. We had to build one from scratch.

The mosque gave us our scaffolding.

Before the Islamic Center of Greater Toledo opened in 1983, the Muslim community worshiped in a modest building on East Bancroft Street—functional, improvised, like so many early American mosques. But by the late 1970s, it was no longer enough. A larger, more diverse congregation had arrived—Pakistanis, Indians, Lebanese, Syrians— bringing not just numbers but a hunger to be seen.

They bought up farmland. They made plans. They wanted more than a building; they wanted permanence. They hired a Turkish architect, Talat Itil, whose design blended the aesthetics of Ottoman domes with the scale of the American Midwest. The result: a 40,000-square-foot structure of white brick, topped by a dome that refuses to collapse into metaphor. It is simply there—full and expansive.

Inside, we stitched together a new kind of belonging. The weekend school was part religious instruction, part cultural negotiation. Our teachers gave lessons in the Prophet's life, while we passed notes about pop songs and movies. We held fashion shows and poetry nights in the multipurpose room. There were Girl Scouts, bake sales, whispered crushes in the hallways.

The cafeteria became our town square. We sat for hours over Styrofoam plates of kibbeh and zaatar bread, learning how to speak across generations and accents. We grew up in English, joked in broken Urdu, dreamed in a syntax that didn't quite belong to either.

The mosque taught us the slow choreography of coexistence. It also taught us to pay attention.

When war broke out in Bosnia, we welcomed refugees into our congregation. Later, Afghans and Iraqis arrived. Palestinians had long been part of the fabric. After 9/11, we stood on uneasy ground, watching suspicion coil around us. But we stayed. We spoke out. We made room. And when other communities—Jewish, Sikh, Hindu—faced their own moments of scrutiny, we stood with them too.

This wasn't just resilience. It was civic formation, brick by brick.

I think about that now, when people talk about leaving the United States. Over the past two decades, I've heard it more often—friends, colleagues, even strangers at dinner parties, fantasizing about other passports, safer shores. Sometimes it's fear that drives the fantasy. Sometimes it's grief. Sometimes it's boredom dressed up as principle.

I understand it. But I'm also wary. Because I grew up in a place where departure was never just a personal choice. It was an event, a rupture. And because I learned something at the mosque that stayed with me: presence matters more than preference.

This country isn't static. It doesn't stay one thing for long. And while its arc may not bend automatically toward justice, it responds—slowly, unevenly—to pressure, to labor, to staying power.

Leaving is one answer. But so is staying. Especially when staying means speaking, insisting, showing up again and again, even when the room grows cold or hostile.

We live in fractured times. Institutions wobble under the weight of contradiction. The loudest voices are often the least curious. We're tempted to disappear into our corners—to retreat into the comfort of the like-minded. But democracy was never supposed to be a quiet agreement. It's a loud, messy, unfinished conversation.

What remains to us, in this moment, is not clarity. It's commitment.

That doesn't mean grand gestures or perfect principles. It means tending to the places we've built—our schools, our neighborhoods, our libraries, our sanctuaries. It means recognizing that civic life doesn't start with elections or end with outrage. It begins with the slow work of listening. It continues in disagreement. It survives in the fragile, necessary muscle of trust.

The Islamic Center of Greater Toledo isn't just a place of worship. It's where I learned that staying is not passive. It's an act of insistence.

I still think about those minarets—how they stand in the middle of the fields, tall and improbable. They don't explain themselves. They just remain. A quiet architecture of belonging, of presence. A reminder that we are here. And that we're not leaving. ★

Time for a New Synthesis

Americans yearn for shared purpose. But we are trapped
in an archaic and badly designed political system that
fractures us by our differences instead of uniting us by
common values. To find the way out, we need to change
how and where we come together to get things done.

BY MICAH L. SIFRY

Co-founder, Civic Hall and Personal Democracy Forum

I am an American Jew and the son of a Holocaust survivor.
My mother was born in Belgium in the early 1930s and, along with her
family, tried to flee to Britain when the Nazi army overran their country
in 1940. By the time they made it to the coast, the Germans had already
captured the port city of Ostend. My mother survived the Nazi occupa-
tion separated from her parents, hidden in a convent and at other times
in homes of members of the Belgian Resistance. Her family was lucky.
My wife's father also lost many family members; she carries a copy of a
list he made of more than 80 of them.

I think of this heritage often, more so now as we face the rise of
authoritarianism in America. Experts on how democracies collapse say
they not only see all the warning signs here, but they are also shocked
at how quickly norms and institutions are falling to Trump's assault.
Sometimes, while catching up on the latest news and feeling my inherited

epigenetic trauma, I wonder if I should leave America, the country where I was born. And then I think, no. We have to stand and fight here.

Indeed, if we take America's history seriously, this fight isn't a new one.

But we need to also stop addressing our problems in isolation from each other and treating them with short-term Band-Aids rather than long-term cures. That's why I believe that we need a new synthesis—a way of doing politics that doesn't divide us by our differences, but that unites us by our common values.

The core tension of America's ongoing democratic experiment is ensuring majority rule without enabling the tyranny of the majority. The Founders deliberately dispersed power among the three branches of government, reserved many powers for the states, and gave the White male landowning (and slave-owning) minority extraordinary advantages in everything from apportionment of population to the design of the Senate. Another, more critical, view argues that the Founders never intended for America to be a nation where all people were equal, and therefore sought to accentuate the power of the propertied minority to be able to block the demands of any putative majority.

However one sees the Founders' intent, the development of actual democracy in America can best be understood as an ongoing contest between an organized minority (the propertied class) and a disorganized majority (the rest of the people).

At various moments in our history, ordinary people have organized themselves sufficiently against the advantages of that powerful minority to win meaningful improvements: abolition, women's suffrage, direct election of senators, child labor bans, income tax, collective bargaining, occupational safety laws, the Voting Rights Act, environmental protections, abortion rights, gay rights, and campaign finance regulations that began to limit private spending on politics, to name a few.

And at various moments in our history, the propertied class has fought back in a number of guises—the slavocracy (aka the "Slave Power"), the robber barons, Jim Crow, the monied class that Theodore Roosevelt called the "malefactors of great wealth," the New Right, the one percent,

MAGA, and now, the tech broligarchs. The struggle between advocates of an expansive, inclusive democracy and defenders of a narrow, exclusive plutocracy has been with us for a long time.

Remember how we got to today's democratic crisis. Over the last 20-plus years, the Supreme Court has turned back the clock on decades of progress. Minority group voting rights were drastically weakened. Campaign finance rules were eviscerated. Most recently, the Court invented a new kind of immunity for the head of the executive branch. The Republican-controlled Congress is on the verge of giving up the last vestiges of its power to hold the executive in check.

At the same time, the ways that Americans come together to navigate life and make meaning of the times have also changed. The rise of the Internet has undermined mainstream mass media, ravaged traditional local newspapers, and given everyone a personal megaphone and the ability to "do their own research" to construct whatever reality they like. The founders of our great social media platforms thought that they were making the world better by connecting everyone to everyone else, but the result was the fostering of echo chambers and the deepening of social divisions.

Civil society, the great engine of social change, has become warped in similar ways. Older mediating institutions like churches, unions, and neighborhood clubs have grown weaker, as personal fandoms grew stronger. While more Americans than ever before may now participate in the public arena by posting, sharing, commenting, and liking each other's content, we are less connected to our actual physical neighbors and more organized into polarized virtual camps.

Trust in institutions was already in decline thanks to shocks like the Vietnam War and Watergate. The Great Recession of 2008 and the Great Pandemic of 2020 damaged trust even more. And then the most talented demagogue in modern American history came to dominate the stage, preying on people's fears and resentments. The organized MAGA minority has seized control of one of our two major parties, and with that they are governing unchecked, imposing their vision of America on the rest of us.

★

Today we are arguably at, or approaching, the nadir of self-rule in America. Indeed, one major problem for would-be defenders of democracy in 2024 was the perception that they were not interested in improving the system—they cared more about maintaining a status quo that most voters hate. Supermajorities regularly tell pollsters that the American political system needs major changes, including a healthy plurality who want it completely reformed. According to Gallup, public satisfaction with "how democracy is working in this country" has been trending downward since 1998, hitting an all-time low in early 2025. The threads that weave us together as a people are badly frayed.

We cannot win the future from a defensive crouch. It is time to think anew about what has worked in the past to enable ordinary people to claim their share of the American birthright. We need a new synthesis.

Simply put, politics is how we decide who gets what. It's how we resolve differences without recourse to violence. And one utterly crucial if insufficiently appreciated truth about any functioning democracy is this: *Politics is a team sport, not an individual one.* It's worth reminding ourselves that each individual voter has very little power. What matters more than anything is how we use "the power to combine," which Alexis de Tocqueville divined as the heart of America's vibrant public arena, to come together in common purpose.

We have a lot to rebuild. The path to a better future can only run through revived political party organizations and the plethora of secondary associations that help individuals act more sensibly and forcibly in the public arena. Political parties that recruit and elevate candidates and organize voters around common labels and values, and secondary associations that bring people together around shared interests, are the warp and woof of democracy. No healthy democracy exists without them. Reformers who hope to weaken the influence of parties or interest groups are making a gigantic systemic mistake. We will not bowl alone or click ourselves or rank individual candidates to democracy.

Thus one key starting point for starting afresh should be: How and to what degree might changes to our political system incentivize and enhance the ability of the citizenry to participate in self-governance in ways that reknit our frayed social ties?

Three quick answers:

First, it's long past time that we committed ourselves to moving America off the two-party system and onto the path of becoming a pluralistic multi-party democracy, like nearly every other functioning democracy in the world. It's understandable why Americans are so angry and alienated from the political system we have now. The two-party system, where the only way to reject one party is to embrace the other, is stifling the kind of healthy competition that would arise if more parties could meaningfully contend for power.

Today's system, which for all practical purposes forces all political discontent to flow through only two channels, is making both parties raise the stakes of every election. We are caught in an ever-worsening "doom loop," as political scientist Lee Drutman cogently argues. To get to a multi-party system, we need to change the rules so that new parties can form and compete for votes without being forced into the role of the spoiler. Either we enable fusion voting (where two or more parties can nominate the same candidate and thus form broad multi-party coalitions) or we move to multi-member districts where more than two parties can win a representative share of power. Trying to solve America's political crisis without addressing how the existing two-party system keeps making it worse is a fool's errand.

Second, we need to change how we engage with voters (something that more competition from more parties would help spur). The election of 2024 triggered a big debate on the losing side about what lessons need to be learned, between those who argue that Democrats have become too liberal or "woke" and those who say Democrats abandoned the working class and became too "corporatized." While there are bits of truth on both sides, this debate avoids the deeper lesson of 2024, which is that *the way* Democrats do politics is too disconnected from the lives of the people they want to reach. Digital political technology and data has made it very easy and profitable for candidates as well as advocacy organizations to extract money or time (from volunteers). But hollow parties that rely on strangers talking to strangers to beg for their votes, and organizations that are "heads without legs" cannot possibly meet the hunger for connection and meaning. Republicans and their allies benefit from year-round community engagement that occurs at places like evangelical churches and gun clubs; a healthier and more authentic Democratic party (as well as new parties) can only emerge from similar place- and meaning-based hubs.

Finally, the best way to reverse the decline in social trust is to invest heavily in civic infrastructure dedicated to bringing Americans together *locally* in common endeavors. As sociologist Eric Klinenberg discovered when Chicago was hit by an intense heat wave in the summer of 1995, fewer people died in poor neighborhoods that had more social infrastructure—a local park, a thriving church, a shopping strip. That's because people in those areas were more likely to know and care about each other, and consequently to check up on elderly shut-ins who were at greatest risk of dying in the heat. As climate upheaval worsens, the need for local connective social infrastructure will only grow.

Given the immediate challenges facing the rule of law in America today, it's tempting to set these problems aside and try to fight incipient fascism from within the systems that we have. But it's my contention that the more Americans live in civic deserts, spend their time in virtual silos, and experience politics as a hyper-polarized zero-sum game, the more they will be attracted to demagogues and strongmen blaming scapegoats and promising easy solutions. Not only are our nerves frayed, our social fabric is, too. It's time we saw all these separate challenges as different faces of the same problem and gave the work to reknit America together a unifying name. It's time for a New Synthesis. ★

Fusion of Horizons: Democracy, Identity, and the Art of Holding Differences

When we embrace universalism, when we invite those with different perspectives to engage in genuine dialogue, we forge a path toward a new, common future.

BY ILYSE HOGUE

Co-founder of Catalyst for American Futures
and fellow at New America

I am not a philosopher, but I do love ideas. I've always been drawn to what I perceive as a spiritual pursuit of exploration and debate. I grew up Jewish in the long shadow of the Holocaust, where the pursuit of ideas ran a distant second to striving for economic security and social safety. So, activism became my religion. Put off by the imposed objectivity of academia, I left after completing my master's degree in ecology and dove headlong into the world of building movements: movements for equality, movements for freedom, and—above all—movements to advance the promise of liberal democracy.

In the last 10 years, I have felt the movements that I spent my life building buckling and breaking under the dual pressures of encroaching tyranny and a retrenchment in identity politics. What started as the left's valiant attempt to throw off the yoke of White patriarchal rule resulted in a tribalism that spliced and diced the majoritarian coalition into pieces. An ascendant authoritarian right, attuned to exploiting fault lines, invested in the tools and strategies to exacerbate the divides. Caught in the vise grip of past oppression and future tyranny, coalitions imploded, organizations became paralyzed, and society became balkanized at the very moment when our democracy demanded a united front to survive. Delighted by our inability to transcend our differences to move towards the promise of a multiracial democracy, the right now flaunts its bigotry and xenophobia as a feature, rather than a bug.

America's promise of a pluralistic, multiracial democracy is on the line and demands new ideas and new visions.

In my own exploration, I read some early writings of universalists on the origin story of our nation. *E Pluribus Unum*: Out of Many, One. A political application of universalism holds central that certain principles or values apply to all people and cultures, regardless of any specific context. It emphasizes that inalienable rights, intrinsic knowledge, and need for justice are universal traits inherent to being human. While I found it tantalizing in theory, I was skeptical about the possibility of applying a unified framework to disparate communities for whom erasure is a literal threat and assimilation can feel like annihilation.

Then one sleepless night, I stumbled upon the works of Hans-Georg Gadamer. I was particularly taken with his concept of "fusion of horizons"—the idea that when people with different perspectives engage in genuine dialogue, the result is a new understanding that transforms both of them.

Gadamer produced his most famous work, *Truth and Method*, in 1960, when he was 60 years old. He was a German philosopher whose life spanned the Weimar Republic, the rise of Nazi fascism, the Cold War, and the reunification of the country he called home. Some of his critics assert he was accommodating of the Nazi regime; while the evidence is thin on that front, there's certainly no record that he was an active resister.

That point alone would discredit him in the eyes of many, including my younger self. But his complicated history is part of what intrigued me to dig deeper.

Gadamer interacted intimately with events that would shape my life in their aftermath. I know I only exist because my great-grandfather had the courage to leave Eastern Europe after World War I in search of new horizons. He traveled first to Argentina, simply because that was the ticket he could get. After seven years working his way through South and Central America, he crossed the border to the promised land—the United States of America—and settled in El Paso, Texas. My origin story was never when my mom met my dad, although that's a good story. I was always aware that I exist because Papa Benito—as he came to be known through his travels—got out before the cancer of Naziism that was the backdrop of Gadamer's youth metastasized. In the binary of my child-hood, there were those who left and those who perished.

As a Jewish child growing up in Texas, my upbringing was in many ways indiscernible from the other White, middle-class kids who swarmed the malls on weekends. My parents were on solid footing financially, and lived in one of the homogeneous neighborhoods of upwardly mobile sub-urban families.

But we were different. For starters, most of those kids weren't raised on stories of mass genocide and mass mourning. Antisemitism was a boogeyman that would pop up on the playground when a game of tag would make way for an interrogation about why I had killed Jesus. The local country club didn't allow Jews, so the weekly dances attended by my peers were off limits to me. These petty grievances were a far cry from the persecution of my ancestors, but they were constant reminders to not get too comfortable in the proverbial melting pot of eighties America.

We lived a bifurcated existence. My parents struggled to send my sister and me to an upscale private school for girls, where we knew that blending into our classes was important to get ahead. After school, how-ever, we were routed three times a week to the synagogue, where we stud-ied with other kids who were the "onlys" in their schools. We spent our summers at a Jewish sleepaway camp that aggregated kids from families across the South and the Midwest, where the diaspora ranks were thin.

My destiny—my very survival—was tied up in getting the balance between tribalism and assimilation pitch perfect. I dreaded the approach of the Jewish High Holidays, when my absence from school would call attention to my difference. The worst was when they collided with the pinnacle of Texas social life, Homecoming. At Christmas the darkness of our house alone spoke volumes on a block alive with lights and festooned with decorations. I grew used to the social pains that accompanied those small acts of defiance to assimilation. I understood from a young age that the "otherness" was required to prevent a secondary annihilation to the generation of Jewish Americans after the Holocaust: the loss of the distinct identity that so many had died for.

It wasn't until I was able to leave Texas for college and expand beyond my personal horizons that I understood my personal struggle to be a core thread of American mythology. That convergence of pain—of people fleeing persecution, of those forced here through bondage and slavery, of those native to this soil who faced persecution by the newcomers—is woven into the DNA of this country, commingling at the cellular level with the promise of new horizons, new visions, and new futures. America's experiment in multiracial democracy has made it a unique and crucially important experiment in what unites and what divides. The work of our time is to figure out how to heal a fractured nation, full of pain and entrenched self-interest.

Gadamer discerned truth as an event, not a fact. In this worldview, truth cannot be derived from objective observation; it only comes from intentional engagement with others that leaves both parties changed. That truth and transformation occurs when individual horizons—the unique experiences that shape a person and a people—are fused. In that way, Gadamer's version of truth mirrors the natural world, where fragmented ecosystems are in peril and those composed of monocultures collapse. It is only through the interconnectedness of distinct beings that evolution can occur.

Philosophy is clean. Life is messy. The authoritarian takeover in our country did not start with the government or even with policies, although those are important. It started with an idea: that to concentrate power in the hands of a few, the many would have to be divided. They could fragment the ecosystems that we had taken pains to build over decades of work. Their strategy is the perversion of *E Pluribus Unum*—take one and make them many. Limit our horizons, shrink our ecosystems, collapse our vision.

I cut my teeth on activism in the streets during the World Trade Organization protests in Seattle in 1999. Teamsters marching arm in arm with environmental activists dressed as sea turtles became the iconic image for a unified force. We had gathered to fight a corporate cabal designed to supplant the decision-making of sovereign nations on everything from environmental regulations to labor standards. Later, the rallying call of "another world is possible" rang through the years after 9/11 and morphed into the hope and change that brought the Obama coalition together. The promise of unified action resulting in a better world was heady. At MoveOn, I struggled to channel that force into better healthcare, consumer protections, and the bread and butter of what government could deliver to the people. But the Tea Party was ascending, and disinformation abounded.

At the end of Obama's first term in 2012, I had landed at NARAL Pro-Choice America, which I led for almost a decade. I was deeply immersed in how a creeping right-wing authoritarianism manipulated real and manufactured tensions to keep constituencies at odds with each other in order to accrue and maintain power. I also witnessed a growing adherence on the left to a rigid hierarchy of oppression as a means of enforcing power in a divided democracy. What started as an experiment in asserting the dignity of all humans had morphed into a culture committed to endless segmentation—in a moment that required connection and collaboration. I saw democracy teetering on the edge, distrust and disengagement growing, and worlds shrinking.

★

The shock of October 7 forced me into a new reality. I watched my own loved ones turn inward against a perceived indifference to Jewish humanity. I saw deep pain in Muslim communities that bore witness to the horrific war against loved ones in Gaza. I saw the immolation of coalitions and relationships that had been forged over decades. I saw a left where the justification of murder and rape became mainstreamed. I saw the right, riddled with antisemites, delight in the weaponization of my people's pain for further evisceration of the rules and laws that govern a liberal democracy.

I vividly remember sitting in synagogue on the High Holidays a year after that horrific inflection point. A parent of a hostage who was still being held pleaded with our congregation: To see his child safely returned to us required us to see the universal anguish of the Palestinian parents who were losing children daily in the war. My rabbi gave a moving sermon on the dual requirements of our faith to invest in universalism and particularism: being able to hold the whole of humanity while asserting our unique identity. I looked to forge the corollaries in my political spaces.

Gadamer's fusion of horizons feels both nearer and farther than ever before. And yet, this was the life force of his work—not the idea that we should transcend our differences, our distinct identities and experiences, but that we need to lean into them. While our interpretations of events may differ, our ability and desire to interpret is universal to human experience. And through that process of shared interpretation, we can transform reality without losing what is uniquely ours.

Introducing the idea of universalism at a moment of deep fracturing can feel quaint at best and scary at worst. A perverted version of universalism has been used to promote erasure and enforce conformity. A modern universalism is imperative for survival, but it must embody the lessons of the last century. Universalism, much like our Constitution, will fail if it assumes a static endpoint. People cannot, and should not, accept the rote musings of founders and philosophers. Like the fight for a more perfect union, modern universalism must embody an ongoing process—one that is forever fusing horizons.

Actively seeking a fusion of horizons cannot be replaced by seeking consensus, which too often reduces differences to the lowest common denominator. Nor can it minimize or transcend the intergenerational pains and the triumphs that connect us to a greater sense of meaning and place in the world. And finally, it cannot be about asserting the primacy of one interpretation of the past over all others.

Approaching the concept of fusion as an ethical mandate can power a political universalism purpose built for this fragmented moment. We can forge a new social contract that centers curiosity and openness, sees validity in multiple perspectives, and honors the meaningful connections that come from engaging through difference. And most of all, we must be comfortable with tension—not the tension of never being absolved of past sins or the tension of trying to be invisible in the face of repression, but the tension of holding onto the familiar while being comfortable with the strangeness of birthing something new.

I ended up marrying someone who is not Jewish, which would not have pleased Papa Benito had he lived to see the day. It comes with some tension, but I'm still Jewish. My husband and I have both transformed through our fused horizons. Our kids are able to hold both of their rich heritages as distinct but intertwined pieces of their whole selves. They are my daily living proof that if we trust the space between assimilation and tribalism, we can pursue a universalism that is not one or the other, but a third, more perfect union of the two. ★

The All-American Movement: Strengthening and Saving Democracy

The rise of tribalism has undermined Abraham Lincoln's universalist vision. There are specific steps we can take to create a unifying agenda for our next 250 years.

BY JOHN AVLON

Journalist, author, and historian

Universalism. It's a big word for a simple idea: the belief that there is far more that unites us than divides us.

This common sense is uncommon today. We are surrounded by divisive appeals online and in the political arena, but for all our interesting differences, we are all Americans and we have shared values. Especially in divided times, we need to lean into those common values to find common ground.

This is not a call for a kumbaya caucus that ignores our dangerously divided democracy. Instead, it is a call to reconnect with our founding values as a renewable source of strength against a hyper-partisan status quo that threatens the success of the American experiment.

From our founding, the United States was a rebellious project: We were the first nation in the history of the world founded upon an idea rather than a tribal identity. That idea, however imperfectly applied, was nonetheless revolutionary. In every generation, we have fought to expand that idea to form a more perfect union.

In the run-up to the 1860 election, Abraham Lincoln explained that "the theory of our government is universal freedom"—making clear that individual liberty and equality were not inevitably in opposition but could act in concert, paving the way for an end to our original sin of slavery.

This belief in universalism was also the underlying logic of the civil rights movement. Dr. Martin Luther King Jr. called for the long-delayed passage of civil rights and voting rights legislation a century after the Civil War by framing it as a fulfillment of our nation's first principles. He made a patriotic case for progressive change rooted in our founding ideals, which helped build a broader coalition to support what had been so long resisted. He said the goal was to "transform the jangling discords of our nation into a beautiful symphony of brotherhood."

There has, of course, been longstanding opposition to the idea of universalism. This is often rooted in an "us vs them" nationalism that is decidedly different from American patriotism. I wrote about one early incarnation of this appeal in my book *Lincoln and the Fight for Peace*:

> "They were elites posing as populists, driven by fear of de-mographic change. Building a 'blood and soil' appeal to racial and regional identity, their anxiety grew as the nation grew... Sometimes this meant cloaking their interests in grand consti-tutional arguments about states' rights. Increasingly, on the floor of Congress, it meant threats of violence while playing the vic-tim—a tactic known as 'aggressive defensiveness'... They claimed that their state's right to slavery was a question of liberty. Twist-

ing logic even further, they argued secession was a form of patriotism because they put loyalty to their state ahead of the nation. They felt judged by outsiders who did not understand their way of life. They reacted to this perceived hate with hate."

Tribal politics are a kill shot to our country, and this antebellum form ultimately escalated into the Civil War. As Mark Twain is reputed to have said, history doesn't repeat itself but it often rhymes. Today we can hear the echoes of this populist nationalism in arguments far removed from issues of slavery and secession.

But universalism also has its critics from the far left in modern American politics. This form of identity politics tries to divide society into competing groups based on superficial differences, breeding a politics of resentment and mutual incomprehension that elevates grievance over equal justice under law. It suffocates reasoned debate, presuming that individuals are guilty of societal crimes unless they prove themselves innocent in some sort of struggle session. The ideological litmus tests become suffocating, demonizing disagreement. The pursuit of tolerance comes intolerant.

There are lots of problems with this. It is illiberal and alienates more people than it attracts. More importantly, it ignores the fact that much of the evil in the world comes from seeing and judging people as members of groups rather than as individuals. It also undercuts the idea that democracy depends upon an assumption of goodwill among fellow citizens.

The only way out of this worsening pendulum swing of hyperpartisan polarization is to resist the politics of "us against them," which is the opposite of our national motto, *E Pluribus Unum*—out of many, one. We need a new All-American movement that focuses on what unites us.

Building such a movement requires defining common ground and then building on it. It requires the courage to challenge the hyperpartisan status quo and stand up to illiberalism on the far right and far left. We can do this in good conscience and with a deep sense generational of purpose, because we have an urgent goal: to strengthen American democracy for the twenty-first century.

After all, it's not an accident that authoritarian competitors abroad keep trying to inflame America's divisions at home. They understand that democracy is discredited when we are divided and dysfunctional. We need to take this challenge seriously and present an alternative that appeals to American patriotism and advances unifying policies.

A few years ago, I co-authored an essay called "The Unum Test" with my friends Jonathan Haidt, Maya MacGuineas, and Mickey Edwards. It proposed a series of reforms determined not by what party had put them forward but instead by whether the downstream effect would unite the nation or further fragment us.

We advocated political reforms such as redistricting reform, open primaries, and ranked choice voting—because these changes would shift the twisted incentive structure that moves power from the problem-solving middle to the partisan extremes.

In addition, there is now an evident need to rein in the excesses of executive power to restore the founders' intended separation of powers, (as proposed by Jack Goldsmith) and to consider some of Yuval Levin's ideas on how to reform Congress. Eventually, we may inspire enough courageous and independent-minded political leaders to stand together against the polarized power structure of our two-party system to help bridge our divides.

But political reforms are not enough: We also need to focus on economic and cultural reforms if we really want to reunite our nation.

It's not a coincidence that we've hollowed out the middle of our politics at the same time we've hollowed out the middle of our economy. We need to focus on rebuilding a strong and vibrant middle class to address the affordability crisis. That means we need to get back to building again, implementing ideas put forward in the book *Abundance* by streamlining overly burdensome regulations so that we can modernize our infrastructure and re-shore essential manufacturing.

Simplification can also help relieve the burden on small businesses that do not have the ability to compete with the phalanx of lawyers, lobbyists, and accountants deployed by large corporations. The tax code should incentivize creating long-term value through research and development, and profit-sharing with employees to align the interests of management and labor.

★

A nation founded on an idea rather than a tribal identity is uniquely dependent on unifying stories to succeed. But we have eroded civic standards that teach the responsibilities of citizenship. As George Washington once said, enlightened opinion is necessary for a self-governing society.

We need to restore civic education in our schools to provide a baseline of civic knowledge. As one big step toward that goal, we should require every graduating high school senior to take the same basic exam required of new citizens. In addition, we should pursue an expanded version of national service in exchange for the forgiveness of student debt. This would not just be military service but organizations like AmeriCorps, Teach for America, and the Peace Corps—bringing together young people from diverse backgrounds to teach them the value of service, giving them experiences they can apply to the job market while showing them that there is more than unites us than divides us as Americans.

Finally, we've got to address the fragmenting effect of transformational technological changes. In a rare bit of good news, laws mandating phone-free schools have received broad bipartisan support in an effort to protect teen mental health. Now we need to advance basic guardrails around artificial intelligence and social media algorithms to ensure a degree of transparency and accountability, advancing a fact-based debate while emphasizing that freedom of reach is not the same as freedom of speech.

I mention these specific proposals because it's important to have a unifying agenda to work toward. Talking about solutions is empowering, while fixating solely on problems is exhausting. But successful pro-democracy movements are about channeling people's frustrations in a constructive direction. They are patriotic, positive, and inclusive—recognizing that citizens need to take action to protect democracy, because we cannot wait for someone else to come save us.

An All-American movement would help us transcend the tribalism that divides us. We need it as a sane counterweight to the extreme hyper-partisan polarization that the founders warned was a danger to democracy. There is no silver bullet. We are, as always, imperfect people trying to form a more perfect union. But history has proven that can be enough if the moment is met with a sense of urgency, perspective, and purpose. ★

Contributors

★

John Avlon is an award-winning journalist, author, and historian. He is a former CNN anchor and senior political analyst, editor-in-chief of The Daily Beast, and the 2024 Democratic nominee in New York's first congressional district. Previously, he served as the chief speechwriter for the mayor of New York during the attacks of 9/11. He currently hosts a solutions journalism podcast on The Bulwark called "How to Fix It" and serves as the chairman of Citizens Union, New York's oldest good government group. Avlon is the author of six books, including *Lincoln and the Fight for Peace* and *Washington's Farewell*.

MORE INFORMATION: JOHNAVLON.COM

Shamila N. Chaudhary is a foreign policy professional with extensive experience working at the White House National Security Council, United States Senate, Department of State, and U.S. Agency for International Development. She uses analysis, creative writing, dialogue, and visual arts to explore issues of war, conflict, and identity in U.S. foreign policy. After working for the government on the war in Afghanistan, she left to explore her ideas about policy issues through the creative process. A mostly self-taught multimedia artist, she studied photography at the George Washington University Corcoran School of the Arts and Design, co-edited the documentary photography book *UnPresidented: The Inauguration of Donald J. Trump and the People's Response*, and served as president of the board of directors for *Focus on the Story*. At Johns Hopkins School of Advanced International Studies, she served as executive director of *The Big Picture*, a forum exploring international affairs through arts and culture.

MORE INFORMATION: SHAMILAPHOTO.COM

Sharon Davies is the president and CEO of the Charles F. Kettering Foundation, which advances inclusive democracy around the world by nurturing citizen engagement, promoting government accountability, and countering authoritarianism. She was previously provost and senior vice president for academic affairs at Spelman College and vice provost for diversity and inclusion and chief diversity officer at the Ohio State University. Davies was a member of OSU's Moritz College of Law faculty for 22 years, serving as the Gregory H. Williams Chair in Civil Rights and Civil Liberties and directing the university's Kirwan Institute for the Study of Race & Ethnicity, an interdisciplinary engaged research institute known nationally for its work in social justice, equity, and inclusion.

MORE INFORMATION: KETTERING.ORG

Deepti Doshi is co-director of New_ Public, a nonprofit R&D lab creating healthier, more inclusive digital spaces. She has built her career at the intersection of technology, social change, and local community organizing. As a director at Meta, Doshi launched the Community Partnerships team, working closely with online group administrators to build tools and programs that strengthen digital communities, and helped establish the New Product Experimentation team. She is also the founder of Haiyya, India's largest community organizing platform, which started a local organizing project in her own neighborhood, and previously, she co-founded Escuela Nueva India and The Fellows Program at Acumen. Doshi brings a global, cross-sector lens to building community infrastructure—both online and locally. She holds degrees from the Harvard Kennedy School and the Wharton School of Business, and fellowships at TED and Aspen Institute.

MORE INFORMATION: NEWPUBLIC.ORG

Judy Estrin is a networking technology pioneer, Silicon Valley leader, and the author of *Closing the Innovation Gap.* Currently, as CEO of JLabs, LLC, she is a speaker and advisor in the areas of entrepreneurship, leadership, and innovation. Her more recent writings are focused on the impacts of technology on democracy and society. Since 1981, she has co-founded eight technology companies, served as chief technology officer of Cisco Systems, and served on the boards of Disney and FedEx. She holds a B.S. degree in math and computer science from UCLA, and an M.S. in electrical engineering from Stanford University, where she worked on what became the Internet.

MORE INFORMATION: JLABSLLC.COM

Seth Flaxman co-founded Catalyst for American Futures after leading Democracy Works as its founding CEO for 12 years, scaling a critical resource that continues to provide tens of millions of Americans with trusted election information online. His leadership has been recognized in *Forbes* magazine's "30 Under 30" list, and as a Draper Richards Kaplan entrepreneur, Ashoka Fellow, Aspen Ideas Fellow, and Bluhm Helfand Social Innovation Fellow. Flaxman founded Democracy Works while receiving a MPP at the Harvard Kennedy School and after working at the Council on Foreign Relations. He earned his bachelor's degree at Columbia University, where he was student body president, successfully advocating for the largest expansion of financial aid in the school's history. Flaxman is a seventh-generation New Yorker married to his college sweetheart and is writing a historical fiction novel set in St. Louis, 1861.

MORE INFORMATION: AMERICANFUTURES.COM

Samsher (Sam) Singh Gill is the third president and CEO of the Doris Duke Foundation (DDF), a New York-headquartered, national philanthropic organization working to build a more creative, equitable, and sustainable future through programs in arts and culture, nature, and health and well-being.

MORE INFORMATION: DORISDUKE.ORG

Nils Gilman is the chief operating officer and executive vice president at the Berggruen Institute, in which capacity he directs the day-to-day activities of the Institute, leads its research program, and serves as deputy editor of *Noema* magazine. He has previously worked as associate chancellor at the University of California, Berkeley, as research director and scenario planner at the Monitor Group and Global Business Network, and at various enterprise software companies including Salesforce.com. He is the author of *Mandarins of the Future: Modernization Theory in Cold War America* (2004), *Deviant Globalization: Black Market Economy in the 21st Century* (2011), and *Children of a Modest Star: Planetary Thinking for an Age of Crises* (2024). He holds a bachelor's, master's, and doctorate in history from the University of Calilfornia, Berkeley.

MORE INFORMATION: BERGGRUEN.ORG

Ilyse Hogue is a co-founder of Catalyst for American Futures and a Fellow of Political Reform at New America. Trained as an ecologist, Hogue has put those skills to use in understanding and leveraging systems of power: social movements—both left and right—as well as systems of governance and politics. Her career has spanned issues, diving into opportunities for and barriers to collective and societal progress. As a trained scientist, Hogue has always taken a data-driven and research-grounded orientation to effective strategies to advance social change, honing those skills in her time as a leader at MoveOn.org, where she led the communications and advocacy efforts for the six-million-plus member organization. She spent nearly a decade as the president of NARAL Pro-Choice America (now Reproductive Freedom for All), where she tripled the membership and authored the bestselling book *The Lie that Binds* about the role of abortion in the long-term plan for the authoritarian takeover of America.

MORE INFORMATION: AMERICANFUTURES.COM

Philippa Pham Hughes is a social sculptor and writer whose mission is to create a society in which all humans flourish. She has been a social practice resident at the Kennedy Center, visiting artist for arts and civic engagement at the University of Michigan Museum of Art, and a lecturer at the Ford School of Public Policy at the University of Michigan. She is a contributing author in the forthcoming book, *An Empathy-Building Toolkit for Museums*. She has spoken widely, including at SXSW, the Cato Institute, TEDxAmericanUniversity, Davidson College Center for Civic Engagement, University of Michigan's Penny Stamps Speaker Series, Art & Democracy Day at Hopkins Bloomberg Center, and Fort Worth Women's Policy Forum. Her work has been featured by artnet, CNN, NPR, PBS Newshour, CityLab, and *The Washington Post*. (Headshot photo by Daniel Ribar)

MORE INFORMATION: PHILIPPAHUGHES.COM

Theodore (Ted) R. Johnson is a contributing columnist for *The Washington Post* and senior advisor to the think tank New America. His research and writing primarily explore the role that race plays in electoral politics and democratic culture, and its influence on the national narrative and the American identity. Johnson is a retired U.S. Navy Commander whose service over two decades included service as a White House fellow and speechwriter to the chairman of the Joint Chiefs of Staff. Following his military career, he spent time at Deloitte and the Brennan Center for Justice. He is the author *of When the Stars Begin to Fall: Overcoming Racism and Renewing the Promise of America* and *If We Are Brave: Essays from Black Americana*.

MORE INFORMATION: NEWAMERICA.ORG

Hugh Jones works at the intersection of technology, media, and democracy. He holds a bachelor's degree in political and social thought from the University of Virginia, where he wrote his thesis on how to make social media platforms better spaces for democratic discourse. After graduating in 2021, Hugh helped lead communications and digital strategy at The Welcome Party and

WelcomePAC. He is a self-taught software developer and previously interned at the University of Virginia Center for Politics and the Berkman Klein Center for Internet and Society at Harvard University. With his co-author Hannah Koizumi, Jones is the co-director of Civic Attention.

MORE INFORMATION: CIVICATTENTION.ORG

Jonathon Kahn is a professor of Religion, Africana, and American Studies at Vassar College, and is the former director of Vassar's engaged pluralism project. His scholarship and teaching bridge political theory, religious studies, and ethical reflection and strive to make the tensions at the heart of American pluralistic democracy accessible and alive. He is currently working on a book on American secularism and is the author of *Divine Discontent: The Religious Imagination of W. E. B. Du Bois*, the co-editor of *Race and Secularism in America*, and many book chapters and essays on race and religion in a wide variety of publications. As director of engaged pluralism, Kahn developed on-campus projects that explored what it means to build community through engaging both our commonalities and differences.

MORE INFORMATION: VASSAR.EDU/FACULTY

Hannah Koizumi's expertise lies at the crossroads of data, civic engagement, and organizing. She holds a bachelor's degree in public policy and a master's degree in data science, both from the University of Virginia. The common thread among her work is civic collaboration—from nonpartisan civic engagement at UVa and DoSomething to bipartisan efforts to strengthen American democracy at the Leadership Now Project and Center for Ballot Freedom. With her co-author Hugh Jones, Koizumi is the co-director of Civic Attention.

MORE INFORMATION: CIVICATTENTION.ORG

Jonathan Kreiss-Tomkins is a fellow for the Institute for Responsive Government, a public policy think tank, and a political consultant. He served five terms in the Alaska Legislature from 2012 to 2022, representing his home region of rural Southeast Alaska. Over his five terms in office, Kreiss-Tomkins focused on long-term fiscal policy, fisheries management, and Alaska Native revitalization. He founded Outer Coast College and Alaska Fellows Program and now serves on the board of both organizations.

MORE INFORMATION: JAYKAYTEE.COM

Luis Lozada is the CEO of Democracy Works, a nonpartisan civic tech nonprofit organization working to increase voter participation, support election officials, and deepen America's culture of civic engagement. During his time as CEO, Lozada has overseen the launch of an award-winning elections data API, enabling innovative integrations with TikTok, Anthropic, and Perplexity AI in 2024. Under Lozada's leadership, Democracy Works has also transformed TurboVote into a comprehensive hub for voter guidance used by millions of Americans. TurboVote helps voters preview what's on their ballot, find their polling locations, access registration support, and receive automated election reminders.

MORE INFORMATION: DEMOCRACY.WORKS

Barry C. Lynn is executive director of the Open Markets Institute in Washington and Brussels. Over the last two decades, Lynn pioneered understanding of how the monopolies of the twenty-first century threaten our democracy, individual liberties, security, and prosperity. Lynn's efforts to update antimonopoly law and thinking for the digital era were fully embraced by the Biden administration and the European Commission, and largely embraced by the Trump administration. His warnings on structural flaws in international systems predicted today's supply chain crises, and his proposed solutions have shaped strategy and policy in the U.S. government, Europe, Asia, the IMF, and the OECD. Lynn developed his thinking in three books: *End of the Line* (2005), *Cornered* (2010), and *Liberty from All Masters*

(2020), as well as numerous articles, speeches, and Congressional testimony. Lynn's thinking has been widely profiled, including in *The New York Times* and *The New Yorker*.

MORE INFORMATION: OPENMARKETSINSTITUTE.ORG

Jason Mangone is the executive director of More in Common US. He began his career as an infantry officer in the United States Marine Corps, and since then has been a research associate at the Council on Foreign Relations, director of the Aspen Institute's Franklin Project, and then the COO of Service Year Alliance. He's also worked in New York City government and co-authored the national best-selling book *Leaders: Myth and Reality*, which the *Financial Times* named a "Best Business Book of 2018." He lives in Princeton, New Jersey, with his wife, Kara, and their four kids, where he serves on the board of the Princeton Little League and is a volunteer firefighter and is on the board of New Politics, which recruits and trains military veterans and alumni of national service programs to run for elected office.

MORE INFORMATION: MOREINCOMMON.COM

Mari Manoogian is executive director of The Next 50, which supports the next generation of elected Democratic leaders by developing their leadership capabilities and building their political and fundraising networks. She most recently served as midwest political and coalitions director for the Biden-Harris and Harris-Walz campaigns. In 2018, Manoogian flipped a historically Republican district in metropolitan Detroit and served two terms in the Michigan House of Representatives. In 2020, she served as co-chair of Armenian Americans for Biden and was a keynote speaker for the 2020 Democratic National Convention. Manoogian earned her B.A. and M.A. from the Elliott School of International Affairs at the George Washington University. She is a member of the board of Figure Skating in Detroit, the Meridian International Center's Rising Leaders Council, a Truman National Security Project Political Partner, and member of the Armenian Genocide Education Committee of Michigan.

MORE INFORMATION: THENEXT50.US

Steven Olikara is a nationally recognized changemaker at the intersection of media, politics, and culture. He serves as the founding president of Bridge Entertainment Labs (BEL) and as senior fellow for political transformation at the USC Schwarzenegger Institute. Olikara founded Future Caucus (formerly Millennial Action Project), the largest cross-partisan organization of young elected leaders in the United States. In 2022, he made history as the first South Asian candidate for U.S. Senate in Wisconsin, garnering national attention for his fresh approach to politics. His commentary and analysis have been featured on CNN, NBC News, *The Washington Post, USA Today, Variety,* and more. Olikara's journey is featured in the documentary film *The Reunited States* on Amazon Prime and PBS, and he co-authored the book *JFK: The Last Speech*. A proud Wisconsin native and former radio DJ, he has been named a Truman Scholar, *Forbes* "30 Under 30" in 2017, and a World Economic Forum Global Shaper.

**MORE INFORMATION:
BRIDGEENTERTAINMENTLABS.ORG**

Micah L. Sifry is a writer, editor, and organizer with nearly 40 years of experience covering politics, technology, and international affairs. He is the former president and co-founder of Civic Hall, New York City's collaborative community center for civic tech, which grew out of his 15 years curating the annual Personal Democracy Forum conference. He is also the co-founder of the Civic Tech Field Guide, a living repository of information on more than 11,000 projects, companies, tools, platforms, and processes using technology for the public good. He is the author or editor of nine books and currently writes The Connector, a weekly newsletter on democracy, movements, organizing, and tech.

MORE INFORMATION: MICAHSIFRY.COM

Anne-Marie Slaughter is an academic, author, and global leader and the CEO of the think and action tank New America. She was the first woman director of policy planning in the U.S. State Department under Secretary Hillary Clinton and the first woman dean of Princeton University's School of Public and International Affairs. She also served as the J. Sinclair Armstrong Professor of International, Foreign, and Comparative Law at Harvard Law School and as president of the American Society of International Law. Slaughter has written and lectured widely on foreign policy and global governance, care and gender quality, and American renewal. The author or editor of nine books, Slaughter is a contributing editor to the *Financial Times* and a regular columnist for *Project Syndicate*.

MORE INFORMATION: NEWAMERICA.ORG

Michael J. Sorrell is president of Paul Quinn College in Dallas. With 18 years at the helm, he is not only the longest-serving president in the HBCU's 153-year history, but his tenure is also one of the longest in the country. He is one of the most celebrated college presidents in America and counts among his honors being named by *Fortune* magazine as one of the World's 50 Greatest Leaders and to *Time* magazine's list of the "31 People Changing the South." He was awarded the President George W. Bush Institute's Trailblazer Citation and Higher Education President of the Year by Education Dive. He is also the only three-time recipient of the HBCU Male President of the Year Award. During Sorrell's tenure at Paul Quinn, the college has improved graduation rates by more than 30 percent; reduced the average student loan debt by $30,000; built the first new buildings on campus in 50 years; created the Urban Work College Model; and won the HBCU of the Year and HBCU Student Government Association of the Year.

MORE INFORMATION: PAULQUINN.EDU

Peter Teague co-founded Catalyst for American Futures after nearly 30 years in philanthropy providing strategic advice to foundations, individual donors, and nonprofit organizations. An attorney, Teague has served as a senior strategist and director for national grant-making foundations, senior policy advisor in the U.S. House and Senate, Peace Corps volunteer, and executive director of the eco-modernist Breakthrough Institute and Horizons, the Bay Area's LGBTQ community foundation. Teague has been instrumental in creating and nurturing a number of groundbreaking initiatives, including climate strategies that harmonize economic and environmental resilience with a global clean energy transition. He serves as senior advisor on climate change to funders including the William and Flora Hewlett Foundation. He has also worked with the Hewlett Foundation, Democracy Funders Network, and the Omidyar Network on issues facing American democracy. Teague has spent significant time in Southeast Asia, India, and East Africa focusing on energy access and women as agents of change.

MORE INFORMATION: PTPHILANTHROPIC.COM AND AMERICANFUTURES.COM

Sally Vance-Trembath is a teaching professor of religious studies at Santa Clara University in California. She has worked in Catholic education all her professional life and has been particularly interested in the relationships among the Church, school, and society. During the Vatican's investigation of the liberal Archbishop Raymond Hunthausen, she served on his Pastoral Council. That experience was seminal in the formation of her work on the ecclesiology of Vatican II. She is the author of several academic publications and has served as national vice president of Voice of the Faithful, the lay organization that was formed to respond to the abuse of children by clergy and the leadership crisis in the Church. She has appeared frequently on television and radio to talk about Catholic issues.

MORE INFORMATION: SCU.EDU/CAS

Eric K. Ward is one of America's leading voices on the intersection of authoritarianism, hate-fueled violence, and the fight to sustain a multiracial, inclusive democracy. He serves as executive vice president of Race Forward and is a senior fellow at the Southern Poverty Law Center. In a career spanning nearly 40 years, Ward made history in 2021 as the first American awarded the prestigious Civil Courage Prize. His bold, widely cited essay, "Skin in the Game: How Antisemitism Animates White Nationalism," helped reshape the national conversation on antisemitism and is considered a cornerstone in understanding the recent rise in racial authoritarianism in the United States. Ward serves on the boards of the National Committee for Responsive Philanthropy, The Proteus Fund, and Auburn Theological Seminary.

MORE INFORMATION: RACEFORWARD.ORG

Scott Warren, a fellow at the SNF Agora Institute at Johns Hopkins University, leads an initiative focused on exploring, researching, and convening a pro-democracy conservative agenda in the United States. He also leads Local Policy Lab, an initiative supporting cities in engaging residents on democracy and climate policy, teaches courses on Democratic Erosion and Social Entrepreneurship, and has supported efforts to integrate global and domestic democracy policy. He is the founder of the national civics education organization Generation Citizen and the author of the 2019 book *Generation Citizen: The Power of Youth in Politics*. His writings have been featured in *The New York Times, Newsweek, Time, The Wall Street Journal*, the *Christian Science Monitor, Education Week*, the *New York Daily News*, Huffington Post, *San Diego Union Tribune, Sports Illustrated, Philadelphia Inquirer*, and the *Providence Journal*.

MORE INFORMATION: SNFAGORA.JHU.EDU

Acknowledgements

★

In this time of crisis, America needs a movement driven not only by an effective counter-authoritarian strategy but also a compelling vision of a liberal democratic future.

The authors who volunteered their time and talent to this project have helped remind us that while that vision must be fully relevant to twenty-first-century realities, it must also be firmly anchored in America's core universalist values. They worked quickly and diligently to bring this volume to life, and we owe them a great debt of gratitude.

We are also indebted to our fiscal sponsor, Global Impact, and the friends and funders of Catalyst for American Futures, the organization we are building to support the larger pro-democracy effort. This work would not have been possible without them.

We are fortunate to have had the skillful assistance of a fantastic team of professionals including designer Shannon Ryan of Made with Relish, LLC; legal counsel Nicholas Arons of Katsky Korins, LLC; and American Futures COO Vince Errico.

Huge thanks to editor par excellence Roseann Foley Henry, who quickly understood our vision and worked to realize it with uncommon patience and good humor.

Finally, we are grateful to our friends and family, who have been generous and loving when we have been harried and distracted.

Thank you all.

www.ingramcontent.com/pod-product-compliance
Lightning Source LLC
Chambersburg PA
CBHW051309120626
46547CB00015B/2151